Dedication
For Lawrence Phillips

Contents

Front cover: Emma painted by J Schmidt, Nelson's favourite depiction of her. See plate 33.

Copyright © Barry Gough 2016
'That Hamilton Woman' essay © Estate of Arthur Marder 2016
Introduction copyright © Andrew Roberts 2016

First published in Great Britain in 2016 by
Seaforth Publishing,
Pen & Sword Books Ltd,
47 Church Street,
Barnsley S70 2AS

www.seaforthpublishing.com

British Library Cataloguing in Publication Data
A catalogue record for this book is available
from the British Library

ISBN 978 1 4738 7563 0 (HARDBACK)
ISBN 978 1 4738 7565 4 (EPUB)
ISBN 978 1 4738 7564 7 (KINDLE)

Typeset and designed by MATS Typesetting, Leigh-on-Sea
Printed and bound in Malta by Gutenberg Press Ltd

That HAMILTON WOMAN

Emma and Nelson

Barry Gough

Including the essay *That Hamilton Woman*
by Arthur Marder

Introduction by Andrew Roberts

Seaforth
PUBLISHING

THAT HAMILTON WOMAN

'People will be very sorry they spoke so cruelly of me. One day they will see that they were abusing a tragic figure.'

Susan Sontag, writing of Emma. *The Volcano Lover: A Romance* (1992)

'It is strange to observe how the unfortunate Emma mingles herself with the life of Nelson. The student cannot get away from her. She is as a strand in the rope of his career, and makes herself as much a portion of his later life as if she had been a ship or a battle.'

W Clark Russell, *Pictures from the Life of Nelson* (1897)

List of Illustrations

Introduction

The 1941 classic movie *That Hamilton Woman,* starring Laurence Olivier as Horatio Nelson and Vivien Leigh as Emma Hamilton, was made in Hollywood by the great Hungarian-American film producer Alexander Korda. It was boycotted by the isolationist, anti-war America First Committee when it was released for its obvious propaganda overtones, such as the moment when, hearing of Napoleon's peace offer, Olivier states: 'Gentlemen, you will never make peace with Napoleon ... Napoleon cannot be master of the world until he has smashed us up, and believe me, gentlemen, he means to be master of the world! You cannot make peace with dictators. You have to destroy them – wipe them out!' Small wonder that it was Sir Winston Churchill's favourite film and that he was said to have watched it seventeen times.

Barry Gough has written an excellent overview of the story of the hero and heroine of *That Hamilton Woman,* whose relationship still today constitutes a love affair to stand beside those of Antony and Cleopatra, Romeo and Juliet, Napoleon and Josephine (the last of whom died only eight months before Emma Hamilton). It was an extraordinary tale. One moment Emma was the gorgeous, buxom, rouge-cheeked temptress of the Romney portrait at the Frick Gallery in New York, striking her 'Attitudes' and fascinating a series of upper-class patrons who passed her on from one to the next. Then, after the briefest of interludes as Admiral Nelson's lover, she became a debt-ridden, obese alcoholic eking out her existence in the Calais stews. The tragedy is tangible.

I have an invitation to Nelson's funeral close to my desk, at which ceremony all the eight admirals who carried his coffin at St Paul's Cathedral in January 1806 were in floods of tears. Regency men didn't mind expressing their feelings in a way that their Victorian children and grandchildren felt they couldn't. Yet if Nelson had lived, and become the Duke of Trafalgar, this story would hardly be known today; Emma would have become just another podgy, early nineteenth-century duchess.

Emma's transformation from beloved beauty to destitute has-been was brilliantly told by the distinguished American naval historian Arthur Marder in one of the finest speeches he gave in a long and distinguished career of writing and lecturing, which is reproduced here *in extenso*. Marder rightly emphasises the sheer sex appeal of Lady Hamilton, an essential feature of her personality, but one that Victorian and later writers tended to underplay, out of prudery. One suspects that one of the reasons Regency Society rejected Emma Hamilton was because wives understandably refused to allow their husbands to go anywhere near such a sex-goddess. In recent years the historians Flora Fraser and Kate Williams have followed Marder in rectifying this lacuna in the historical record.

Where Barry Gough does naval historiography a great service in this book is to place Lady Hamilton's story in the wider context of the huge importance of women to the running of the Royal Navy in the age of fighting sail. In what seems at first sight very much an all-male Senior Service, it actually turns out that women were highly important to almost every aspect of the life of the British Fleet, in ways that will surprise readers. Gough's clear admiration for other Nelson historians – Andrew Lambert, Roger Knight, John Sugden, Edgar Vincent and Colin White among them – reminds us that since the Trafalgar bicentenary in 2005 we have been living through a veritable golden age in Nelsonian scholarship. This diligently researched, well written and richly illustrated book, and the superb exhibition at the National Maritime Museum at Greenwich which it complements, are eloquent testament to the continuation of this wonderful renaissance.

PROF ANDREW ROBERTS
Visiting Professor, Department of War Studies,
King's College, London

Preface & Acknowledgements

In bringing Arthur Marder's typescript into print after all these years the publishers have given honour to a great historian and a great subject. The occasion of the special National Maritime Museum exhibition on Emma, Lady Hamilton, on the date of this book's publication, marks a true recognition of Emma's importance in history. *That Hamilton Woman* is the title of the 1941 film, and this too affords us the opportunity of looking at this famous love affair as it has been portrayed on screen. In the movie the son of Fanny Nelson, Josiah Nesbit, then a young naval lieutenant, derisively calls Emma 'that Hamilton woman'. He was loyal to his mother but, having seen all the goings on at Naples, probably lusted after Emma. He was, in the author's opinion, the source of much of the bother. One further point may be made, and it is this: Women have been a central figure in England's rich and remarkable naval history, and in the following text I have given attention to the theme of that yet to be written book 'the women behind the fleet'. Navy wives, mistresses and sweethearts often wore more gold braid than their men, and in Emma, Nelson had his woman behind his fleet. The success at Trafalgar owes more to Emma than has ever been properly admitted, and the National Maritime Museum's attention to this enduring theme is worthy recognition of the importance of 'that Hamilton woman', the smithy's daughter who rose from obscurity to become lover, inspiration and partner of the greatest of Britain's admirals.

I thank Andrew Roberts for his Introduction, the publishers Julian Mannering and Robert Gardiner for producing a beautiful book that befits Emma's countenance, the National Maritime Museum staff for help with the illustrations, the Marder family for permission to publish Arthur Marder's essay, and Amanda Mannering for assistance with Marder's text. Thanks, too, to Peter Hore, Gerald Jordan, Lawrence Phillips, Camilla Turner and Peter Warwick.

What follows is not a biography of Emma or one of Nelson: it is, rather, an extended essay on their interlocking lives, with passing literary portraits of Sir William Hamilton (Emma's husband, the connoisseur and antiquarian) and Frances, Viscountess Nelson (Nelson's estranged wife).

Sources: Writing Emma and Nelson, given at the conclusion of the narrative, is intended to provide the reader with comments concerning some of the materials upon which this book is based. Therein, he or she will find unending prospects for a lifetime of pleasant reading into the enduring love story that here commands our attention and will invite the curiosity of future generations.

BARRY GOUGH, 21 October 2016

Prologue: Arthur Marder's '*That Hamilton Woman*: Emma and Clio Reconciled'

So improbable is the nature of our story that no writer of romantic fiction could fashion such a tale as that of Emma, Lady Hamilton and Admiral Lord Nelson. Truth to tell, all that follows did occur. At the time it was the story of the century, and to this day remains one of the greatest epics of love recorded in human annals.

It is a story of unbridled passion, of a search for fame and for fortune. It cuts to the quick of human emotions. It involves two persons desperately in need of one another's affections and acclaim. In their respective spheres – the one, the necessarily female one, the pursuit of theatrical arts and pleasures; the other, the masculine one, the pursuit of victory at sea in order to secure the safety of the kingdom and the nation – the principals were locked in a strange, but the more we know about it, essential fate that would lead them not only through notoriety and fame but then, at the end of it all, to death and even, in the case of the female, to derision.

Emma and Nelson were moving through time and space towards what they knew must end in pain, separation and disaster. The Battle of Trafalgar brought a finality to the relationship but it only opened to the pages of history unending fascination about two lives brought together in complete and unselfish love, and no matter what may be said about the immorality of their relationship we can say with certainty: 'Here was a love affair for all time.'

So much has been written about Nelson, and rightly so, for England's Glory stands on his own as the greatest of the Sea Kings of England. He was Britannia's instrument, its god of sea battle. As a leader of men, as a strategist and tactician, as a fighting captain, and as a diplomat he stands at the top of the naval profession, and remains today a worthy study of how effective leadership can be attained in military organisations. He is deserving of the superlatives that have been showered upon him. He was vainglorious, he was daring, and at times he was foolish. He led from the front in all things, and was prepared for the consequences. He fought his way upwards in the naval service. He was a rectory admiral, that is he came from one of the families rather common in the Church of England of giving to the Navy one of their sons. He came from humble means and never was a wealthy man. He had aspirations, cut short by his death on 21 October 1805, of some sort of supreme command whose exact dimensions are unclear to us. His death in battle removed him from the scene, bringing immortality just as Captain James Cook's murder at Kealakekua Bay in 1779 or Major General Wolfe's death at the battle of Quebec in 1759 brought them to heroic status beyond the ordinary. Indeed, artists of the age painted scenes of Nelson ascending into heaven just as they had done similarly for Cook and for Wolfe. There was something transcendental in Nelson's passing. He was removed from all the perils and the pains of human existence (which for him were legion) and was raised to a state of freedom from all mortal worries.

At the very end of his life, when breathing his last, he asked that Emma and their daughter Horatia be his legacy to the nation. In his final living moments he was also aware of how inveterate enemies had sought to kill him in battle: 'They have done for me at last', were among his last words. They had, indeed, killed the mortal Nelson but they had given birth to something far more powerful – an imperishable legend and a model for future naval officers.

Emma it was who provided the fire within Nelson in his latter years when scarcely there was anything left of his damaged body – for there he was, all forlorn, without an eye, without an arm, suffering terribly from a hernia and wracked with pain. She was his solace, his adoring companion, his passionate bedfellow and his hope for the future. She fed his vanity. As for herself, she had to fight off other admirers (who made Nelson rage with jealousy), and she had to face the fact that she could not inhabit the same social circles as he could do in polite society. Our admiration for her grows as we realise from what station in life she had come from, how she had survived many a difficult turn in the road of human connections and liaisons, and how she had risen to become one of the finest actresses of her times. She was loved and adored, coveted and acquired – and yet she moved through all passages of her life with grace and self-appreciating acceptance, becoming the lover and confidant of the person upon whose shoulders England's very survival rested. All the same, whereas Nelson rose directly to immortality, Emma declined precipitately into despondency, drunkenness and despair, and she died ten years after Nelson, on French soil – having fled her debtors. Here is one of the saddest of human stories. She commands our attention and our devotion still, and she invites our sympathies. Like many another notable figure that strode the stage of history she was not without fault – money passed all too quickly through her hands, for one thing – and she has had many detractors.

It was these aspects of the interlocking lives of Emma and Nelson that led the famed historian of the Royal Navy, the American Arthur Marder, author of the five-volume classic *From the Dreadnought to Scapa Flow*, to compose a talk and slide presentation '*That Hamilton Woman*: Emma and Clio Reconciled'. Clio, we recall, is the historian's muse, well known to Marder – and

Emma, he confessed, was his mistress. The present writer had the pleasure of listening to Marder give this talk, illustrated handsomely with views of Emma, at an American Historical Association meeting in 1966. It captivated the audience. When, years later, and quite by accident, I discovered the text of it among his documents in the course of writing my book *Historical Dreadnoughts*, the double biography of Marder and his famous sparring partner Captain Stephen Roskill, the famous official historian of British naval events of the twentieth century, I determined to bring this text forward for publication. It shows that Marder had a mistress after all, who was, as he says, Emma. Many illustrations that accompanied Marder's talk are included in this book, most notably those exquisite portraits of Emma by Romney and the James Gillray cruel and unflattering cartoon *Dido in Despair.*

That Hamilton Woman BY ARTHUR MARDER

Every scholar should have one great love, an absorbing passion – a legitimate affair – and one mistress for relaxation. My mistress has been the influence of women on history, for better or for worse, more particularly on naval history. A statement made by Nelson's contemporary, the great Lord St Vincent, caught my attention long ago. 'Wives', pronounced the Admiral, 'will be the ruination of the Service.' This judgement, which was really meant to include mistresses as well as wives, intrigued me, and, after more than three decades of study of the subject, I can state that St Vincent was absolutely right! However, the principal figure in my little talk this evening is an exception: she ruined neither the Service nor her man. And therein lies our story ….

* * *

Antony and Cleopatra, Abelard and Heloise …. Nelson and Emma: the great love stories of history. But contemporaries, historians and biographers have, I am convinced, got the essentials in the last named all wrong ….

The very title of my talk, 'That Hamilton Woman', brings out the fact that Emma, Lady Hamilton was, in her own day, and indeed down to the twentieth century, a much-maligned woman. She was, in her own time, looked down upon by most of English society for making

England's most brilliant fighting seaman a rather ludicrous figure. Admiral Lord St Vincent remarked: 'That infernal bitch Lady Hamilton could have made him poison his wife or stab me, his best friend.' Later, Victorian prudery ensured that her reputation would remain an unsavoury one – even with biographers and historians of repute. Though more recent writers have been kinder, the old attitude lingers on. And so the British reviewer of Dudley Pope's book on Nelson, *England Expects*, writes of Nelson's 'passionate love for a woman as worthless as Emma Hamilton.' The British Official Naval Historian, Captain Stephen Roskill, wrote a few years ago: 'As one reads of the toils in which Nelson enmeshed himself it is difficult not to feel sadness.' This is hardly flattering to Emma! Sir William Hamilton's recent biographer, Brian Fothergill, dismisses her as 'one of the comic characters of English history.' Well, she was something more than that ...

Emma Hamilton was born on or about 26 April 1765 as Amy Lyon, the daughter of a Cheshire village blacksmith and a cook. She did not start as a lady, since she adopted as her profession in her teens that of 'pleasing the gentlemen', as the expression went, while working as a lady's maid, a tavern waitress and so on. Her sole capital consisted of a quite exceptional beauty of face and figure that would later lead to her being classed among the greatest beauties of her age. She was a handsome, becoming woman, with magnificent dark auburn hair. Most men were attracted to her, *sexually* if

not socially. These assets she exploited to the best of her
ability as the means of breaking away from a life of
drudgery. She had a child late in 1781, when she was
living under the protection of a handsome, devil-may-
care baronet, Sir Harry Featherstonhaugh, at Uppark, a
great Sussex estate on top of the Downs above
Portsmouth. (You can still see there the polished
Georgian dining-table on which she was said to have
danced, in a state of nature, for the pleasure of Sir Harry
and his friends. There is, alas, no evidence for the
legend!) Sir Harry kicked her out at this time because
she was noisy and expensive: she had taken to gambling
and drink. Besides, she was about to have her baby, and
Sir Harry had reason to believe he was *not* the father.
On 10 January 1782 the distraught Emma, (Emily Hart
as she was then known) sent an illiterate but heartfelt
scrawl to a friend of Sir Harry's – Charles Greville –
whom she had met at Uppark: '...For God's sake G, write
the minet you get this, and only tell me what to dow ....
I am allmas mad. O, for God's sake, tell me what is to
become on me. O dear Grevell, write to me. Write to me
...' (Her spelling always remained original!)

The Honourable Charles Greville, a younger son of
the first Earl of Warwick and an austerely handsome
bachelor of 33, made Emma his mistress early in 1782.
(He specialised in picking up cast-off mistresses.)
Greville had Amy change her name to the more genteel
Emma. Emma proceeded to fall madly in love with her
mean and conceited patron, and gave herself, body and

soul, to the task of looking after his personal comfort. Greville, to give him his due, treated Emma with kindness and consideration. He had her educated and he made a 'lady' of her – ie taught her the rudiments of ladylike behaviour. He moderated her voice, eradicated the rough edge of her northern accent, calmed her taste in clothes, formed her manners (which included the art of holding a teacup properly and how to comport herself in elegant company), and taught her to sing, play a musical instrument or two, strike classical attitudes, and, in general, to be a credit to him. (With his mercenary outlook, it is possible that he already looked on her as a future asset, for the sale of mistresses was a flourishing trade among the fashionable rakes of the period.) When Emma was presentable, Greville let her be seen. His friends all agreed she was something to look at. Indeed, she was probably the most beautiful woman of her generation: a lovely, girlish face on a beautiful body; violet eyes, heavenly complexion, auburn hair – the lot. The painter Romney went wild over her and painted her in dozens of poses. He was certainly more than a little in love with her himself. Countless pages of sensational fiction have been devoted to lurid accounts of a liaison between the young Emma and the 50-year-old painter. These are utter nonsense. Their relationship was deep and warm, important to both. She was his 'Divine Lady'.

After a couple of years, Greville's uncle, Sir William Hamilton, came into Emma's life. He met her at his favourite nephew's, in 1783, and admired her greatly. Greville, who was far from well off and was hoping to make a rich marriage, planned to sell his mistress to his uncle. Hamilton was a widower, (since 1782) and a pretty decent sort: a man of easy-going temperament – what we today would call 'a very nice man'. He was the owner of one of the finest collections of paintings and antiquities in Europe. (His collection of Greek and Etruscan vases formed the basis of the British Museum's Department of Antiquities.) Unloading Emma on Hamilton was not easy, for she had become deeply attached to Greville, (and was led to believe that Greville would soon follow her out to Naples). But the deed was done. Greville handed her over to Hamilton, who thereupon settled his nephew's debts and made him his heir. The date: 1786. Greville assured his uncle that 'she is the only woman I ever slept with without having ever had any of my senses offended, and a cleaner, sweeter bedfellow does not exist'.

Sir William was Minister to the Court of Naples (i.e. the Kingdom of the Two Sicilies), and in that garish society Emma sparkled. Though she was 35 years younger than her elderly lover, she transferred her fidelity to him without much trouble, once she recovered from the shock that Greville was no longer interested in her and would not join her. In Naples Emma and Hamilton could live openly together without causing scandal. When they went home to London on a visit, in 1791, Sir William surprised everybody by marrying her – quietly in Old Marylebone Church. (She had been after him for five years to do this.)

In 1794, before her affair with Nelson, Emma attracted much admiration in high circles. Her rise on the social scale brought reassuring comment from those who had so much to lose.

'What a charming character L[ad]y Hamilton is', confided Admiral Howe's sister Caroline to Georgiana, Countess Spencer, 'notwithstanding the great disadvantages of her early education, and how different from many who have had every advantage and not allowed themselves to profit from such good fortune.'

Emma became a great friend and confidante of the Bourbon Queen Maria Carolina, Marie Antoinette's elder sister. She began to take part in politics, and by 1795 was, to all intents and purposes, the British Ambassador to Naples, especially since Sir William was ailing. Emma made Hamilton an admirable, affectionate wife. She always had a genuine, if passionless, affection for him. He was highly satisfied with his bargain. To the ageing man she was another acquisition to his collection of treasures, and he treated her more as a pleasant toy than as his wife. He encouraged her to learn French and Italian, both of which she came to speak fluently and with a purer accent than she ever acquired in her native tongue.

Though she was still not received by English society, Lady Hamilton made quite a stir among the Neapolitans because of her beauty, naturalness, talent for singing (it reached professional standard – one impresario offered her a London engagement), and posing in decorous classical attitudes. What were these 'Attitudes' for which Emma became renowned? She offered this entertainment at 'home' – the Palazzo Sessa in Naples, a private mansion leased by Sir William, with an uninterrupted view of the Bay from the Castel dell'Ovo eastward to Vesuvius. (Divided into apartments today … in the square called Vico Santa Maria a Capella Vecchia.) They consisted in her posing, generally in dumb show, with the aid of such adjuncts as a shawl and a tambourine, to represent poses from classical sculpture; Sir William directed the lighting effects. There was, for example, her presentation of Agrippina (Nero's mother) bearing the ashes of Germanicus in a golden urn. (He was her husband, probably poisoned by the Emperor Tiberius.) All who ever witnessed Lady Hamilton's Attitudes agreed they were remarkable. These were the days when her features, lit by good health and great vitality, were faultless. Old Lord Bristol, peer and bishop, exclaimed in 1794: 'God Almighty must have been in a glorious mood when he made you!' Emma's beauty and her talents conquered not only the most sophisticated members of society, but also simple Neopolitans who more than once compared her appearance with that of the Virgin Mary.

We have an interesting description of Emma in 1795 in a letter written by a traveller: 'You may suppose her really an extraordinary woman, without education, without friends, without manners, when she came here; she has added to all the outward accomplishments of a woman of education a knowledge of Italian, French and music, which last, with a very fine voice, she executes divinely .... In her Attitudes she exceeds herself, and joins every grace that ever was united to the greatest beauty of face and person.' Only a few aristocratic English travellers complained that she wrecked the illusion whenever she opened her mouth. Recorded Lady Holland: 'Just as she was lying down, with her head reclined upon an Etruscan vase to represent a water-nymph, she exclaimed in her provincial dialect: "Don't be afeard, Sir Willum, I'll not crack your *joug.*" I turned away disgusted.' To anyone free of Lady Holland's accent-snobbery, it must have been irresistible. Surely it was just this – the combination of the classical beauty Romney painted with the irrepressible spontaneity of a funny girl from Merseyside – that made Emma Hamilton enchanting.

By 1798 she had reached the zenith of her powers; she positively exuded personality. Already she was putting on weight; after all, she was 33, and always had a tendency to stoutness, which she lavishly cultivated by means of a healthy appetite.

'Imagine, then,' writes one Nelson biographer, Renalt Capes, 'the woman who greeted Nelson as he landed from the Nile [1798]. A plump, but still beautiful, figure and a face as yet unravaged by the passing of the years. An all-embracing temperament that could achieve anything. All the arts of the *demi-monde* and the *nouveau-riche* combined. A sound understanding of her prey – man. A real spirit of kindness and hospitality. A friendly naturalness touched with vulgarity and flamboyance, calculated to appeal to a nautical mind ... A superabundance of physical and mental courage. A quick intellect that could carry out an instruction carefully and thoroughly; and, finally, the particular chemical affinity that challenged the Admiral's own ardent nature.'

When Captain Horatio Nelson, then nearly 35, on duty with the British Mediterranean Fleet, called at Naples with dispatches for Sir William Hamilton, in 1793, he was entertained by the Hamiltons. Emma made an indelible impression on him, and she began to take an interest in him as a famous captain. The future lovers didn't meet often until Nelson had lost an eye [1794] and an arm [1797], and – later – won world-wide fame by demolishing the French Fleet in Aboukir Bay (the battle of the Nile), on 1 August 1798, which won him a peerage. Lady Hamilton fainted when she heard the news of the action. She wrote to Nelson:

'I am delirious with joy and assure you I have a fever caused by agitation and pleasure. Good God what a victory! Never, never has there been anything half so glorious, so compleat ... No, I would not like to die till I see and embrace the victor of the Nile ... How I glory in the honner of the Country and my Countrymen! I walk and tread in the air with pride, feeling I was born in the same land with the victor Nelson and his gallant band.'

Nelson arrived in Naples in the *Vanguard* some weeks later, in September. The dramatic scene in the ship when Emma (dressed '*à la* Nelson' – in blue, figured with gold anchors) and Nelson met was described by Nelson to his wife as 'terribly affecting; up flew her Ladyship, and exclaiming: "O God! Is it possible?" she fell into my arm more dead than alive. Tears, however, soon set matters to rights … I hope one day to have the pleasure of introducing you to Lady Hamilton. She is one of the *very best* women in this world … She is an honour to her sex … Her kindness with Sir William to me is more than I can express.' This is hardly the sort of letter a husband in full possession of his faculties would write to a wife! He was within a few days of his fortieth birthday; Emma was 33, Sir William, 68.

Nelson, who had received a nasty head wound at the Nile, now lived with the Hamiltons. They took tender care of him at the Palazzo Sessa. The inevitable came to pass. As many patients have done before and since, Nelson quickly succumbed to the charms of his decorative nurse. As far as Emma was concerned, he was a hero, and as such she lavished on him all her natural kindness, accompanied by the adoration of an admirer. Before he was even convalescent, the battle was over; he fell completely and absolutely in love with his hostess, and she with him.

Her surrender cannot have been easy, fond of her husband as she was and living in days when adultery was legally stigmatised and divorce was unobtainable except by Act of Parliament. She had nothing to gain and everything to lose. Her detractors have accused her of selling herself for ambition, to bask in the reflected glory of being a Hero's mistress. But she had basked already, legitimately, in Nelson's glory, and knew that she could never admit openly to an illicit association. She could have remained his platonic friend with no harm to anyone.

It is understandable that she yielded. Sir William was in his late sixties. He had been ailing for years with his liver, had rheumatism, and was on the whole a very tired man. He had probably not been more than an occasional lover to Emma since their marriage. Significantly, Nelson refers to him in their letters as 'your uncle', which is a fair indication of their relationship. The ardour of Nelson, all afire with passionate adoration, glorified by his peculiar, indefinable charm, was impossible to resist. Once again her sense of virtue was overcome.

It was a long siege, and her physical surrender didn't come until 12 February 1799. She was now Nelson's mistress. Sir William either did not see or, more probably, did not care. He was genuinely fond of Nelson – and the one thing he wanted to avoid was making a scene. In February 1799 Emma, Sir William and Nelson set up house together in the Palazzo Palagonia in Palermo, Sicily, where the Court had gone, following a revolution in Naples. 'They say', wrote young Lady Elgin

1. George Romney began painting Emma in 1782. This early work depicts her
in contemporary dress rather than the more usual allegorical
or mythological guises for which she posed. She already radiates
the calm poise of the experienced adventuress.

2. Mrs Cadogan, Emma's mother,
who acted as Emma's housekeeper until she
died in 1810. It is significant that Emma's worst
financial crises occurred after that date.

3. *Little Emma*, painted by George Greville and thought to be a depiction of Emma as a child, though it could be of Emma's illegitimate daughter, possibly by Sir Harry Featherstonhaugh, known as Little Emma.

4. Emma as Nature. This was the first of more than sixty
portraits that Romney painted of Emma. Commissioned
by Greville, probably as a commercial speculation,
it was completed in March 1782.

5. Emma as a Bacchante. Popularly known for their drinking
and acts of abandonment, Bacchantes offered artists,
as here, the chance to display the female sitter
in wilder and more sensual guise.

6. Thought to have been finished by Romney after Emma left
England for Naples in 1786, this painting portrays
a wistfulness felt perhaps more keenly
by the artist than by Emma.

7. Romney described Emma in a letter of 1791 as 'the divine lady ... superior to all womankind', and Ronald Gower, a trustee of the National Portrait Gallery writing 100 years later, commended the artist as 'essentially a painter of womanly charms'; in this portrait she is shown with all the allure of the muse that she had become for him.

8. A rare picture of Emma, From the Nude, and presumed to
be by Romney, was last seen publicly one hundred years ago
and appeared in Julia Frankau's 1911 biography of Emma.

to her mother in the autumn of 1799, 'that there never was a man turned so *vain glorious* (that's the phrase) in the world as Lord N. He is now completely managed by Lady Hamilton.' Lady Elgin found that Lady Hamilton was pleasant, sang remarkably well, and at dinner, quite in an undress, looked very handsome. But Lady Elgin felt humiliated as she watched Nelson's obvious devotion. 'Lord Nelson, whenever she moved, was always at her side.'

Finally, the English Government, reluctantly made aware of the shenanigans, recalled both Nelson and Sir William. All three set off for London together. Rumours of their relationship preceded them. In England, where the *ménage à trois* arrived in November 1800, Nelson having been feted everywhere en route home, the mob shouted hoarse applause; but society whispered, and Nelson's Service friends shook their heads over how the Admiral was making a fool of himself with Lady Hamilton. Lord Minto, as an old friend, visited Nelson in London and declared of Emma that 'the love she makes to him is not only ridiculous but disgusting'. Nelson was heaped with formal honours and financial rewards, but he and Emma were received nowhere. And Nelson (and Sir William) received a crushing snub from the King (George III) at His Majesty's *levee:* the King turned his back on them!

Horatia Nelson was born at the end of January 1801 at 23 Piccadilly, opposite Green Park, where the Hamiltons were living, and was hustled off to a wet nurse. The world in general knew nothing of the event. (Emma's increasing stoutness had concealed the evidence from her friends!) Nelson regarded Horatia as a 'dear pledge of love'. She had a twin sister. There is evidence (Winifred Gérin: *Horatia Nelson, 1970)* that Horatia's twin sister, named 'Emma Hamilton', did live – that Emma had lied to Nelson, telling him that the infant had died. (Why? We don't know.) It seems likely this other child was handed over to a foundling hospital and survived. A third girl, born early in 1804, did not live long.

It is very probable that the prospect of Lady Hamilton's first child with Lord Nelson was the immediate cause of the rupture between the Nelsons. There was a really dreadful reunion at Nerot's Hotel in King Street, St James's, when Lady Nelson found herself confronted by the returning party. She gave Nelson a deservedly cold reception. Quite apart from the scandalous stories, which had reached her from Italy, the first sight of Emma and her ageing husband side-by-side with her long lost Horatio must have been a terrible shock. When Emma and Fanny now at last met face to face, in November 1800, Emma, in her own words, felt 'an antipathy not to be described'. It was no wonder. Not only was Emma confronted with a rival of impeccable morals, breeding and good manners, standing well with Nelson's old friends, and entrenched in the affection of a father-in-law whom Nelson called 'the very best man that ever I saw', but she was at grips with conventional

English society. Nelson made an attempt to live with Fanny for what remained of that year, 1800, but his position grew progressively more intolerable. Writes one of Nelson's biographers (Oliver Warner): 'He found her refusal to minister to his vanity, her lack of exuberance, even her eloquence and dignity, oppressive; nor, so rumour said, could she altogether forbear to recriminate. It was on the gossip of the newspapers and the insinuations of popular cartoons that she dwelt, not upon the glorification due to the victor of the Nile.'

Early in 1801, her last reserves of patience exhausted, Fanny precipitated the rupture – at the breakfast table, according to the version generally accepted. When Nelson spoke of something that had been done or said by 'dear Lady Hamilton', Lady Nelson rose from her chair and said with much vehemence: 'I am sick of hearing of dear Lady Hamilton, and am resolved that you shall give up either her or me.' Nelson replied calmly: 'Take care, Fanny, what you say. I love you sincerely; but I cannot forget my obligations to Lady Hamilton, or speak of her otherwise than with affection and admiration.' Muttering something about her mind being made up, Lady Nelson left the room and shortly after drove from the house. They never lived together again. But there is another version: that there was no scene, and that they parted with mutual respect and amicably. In any case, Nelson rejected all attempts at reconciliation, and made his home, whenever he was ashore, with the

Hamiltons at Sir William's house in Piccadilly or at Merton, the household expenditure being divided between them.

Fanny remained devoted to her husband, and then to his memory, until her death. Lady Nelson's grand-daughter (by a child of her first marriage) remembered, long afterwards, how Fanny would take her precious miniature of Nelson from its casket – it was one of the few relics she possessed of her husband, apart from his letters. She would look at the miniature affectionately, kiss it, and then turn and say: 'When you are older, little Fan, you too may know what it is to have a broken heart.' She had always behaved most correctly, and she had never failed him, except in a matter which she could not help, that of providing him with an heir.

Nelson's biographers have found it almost impossible *not* to take sides with Fanny or Emma. Fanny, so limited and colourless, has come off poorly, but it was she who deserved pity, for upon Emma was lavished Nelson's burning devotion; it was she with whom his name has been linked in the nation's story.

What about the fourth member of the quadrumvirate? It is most *un*likely that Emma and Nelson deceived Sir William; indeed, it would have been impossible for them to have done so. But appearances were successfully kept up. So far as society was concerned, Sir William remained the unwearyingly doting husband. 'I am,' he wrote to Emma, 'determined that my quiet shall not be disturbed. Let the nonsensical world go on as it will.' He died in his wife's arms, in April 1803, with Nelson's hand in his.

Nelson's last years with Emma, although interrupted by periods of sea service, were his happiest. They lived at the country seat he had in 1801 commissioned her to purchase for him – Merton Place in Merton, Surrey, 'Paradise Merton'. (Of this house and its 70 acres of beautiful grounds, the scene of so much happiness, there is not a trace to be found.) And then came the campaign in 1805 that led to Trafalgar. Emma's reaction to the news of Trafalgar and her hero's death was: 'My heart and head are gone.' Nelson's last letter to her, written on 19 October 1805, two days before his greatest victory, was found on his desk after the battle and was brought to her by Captain Hardy. 'My dearest Emma, the dear friend of my bosom', it began, 'the Signal has been made that the Enemy's combined fleet [that is, the Franco-Spanish fleet] are coming out of port ...' She wrote at the bottom of the letter: 'Oh miserable wretched Emma, Oh glorious and Happy Nelson.'

An old friend told her England would expect a heroic and serene bearing in the confidential friend of the immortal Nelson, and she had tried to assume it. Cynics noticed she went repeatedly to the theatre for the purpose of swooning when the English tenor Braham sang 'The Death of Nelson'. Her efforts at seeming to be happy were hardly more successful and repelled some of her best friends. She entertained a mob of noisy parasites sumptuously at Merton. This, with her support of many poor relations, forced her quickly and deeply into debt. In his will, Nelson had left Emma and his 'adopted' daughter as a legacy to his country – a 'bequest to the nation' – but his embarrassed country would have neither of them. Although Emma had inherited from Nelson and Sir William an income of over £2,000 a year, it soon evaporated. The death of her mother in 1810 removed from her 'the best of Mothers' and the last brake upon her irresponsibility. The final reports of her in England are wholly pathetic. She barely escaped imprisonment for her debt in 1813. In 1814, to escape her creditors, she sailed to France with Horatia and less than £50 in her pocket. She settled in a farmhouse outside Calais; but her last fresh start in life failed. Although she didn't experience actual want, she became an alcoholic (gin and brandy) – and immensely fat, and she fell into debt again, to the point where Horatia, unbeknown to her, wrote to her uncle, Lord Nelson, (Nelson's brother), for a £10 loan. Emma died on January 17th 1815 aged 49. (*NB* Her daughter survived her by many years, dying at the age of 81. She was aware that she was Lord Nelson's daughter, but remained all her life uncertain of the name of her mother. It was a secret which Emma had kept to herself.)

Nelson never disguised his feelings for Emma. To him she was a goddess. He would never check her vulgarity, wince at her noisy voice, or complain of her garish clothes, for he never noticed these defects. To him she was perfect, and they were thoroughly at ease in each other's company. His admiration for the woman he considered perfection, even before she became hallowed in his eyes as the mother of his child, swelled into lyrical language. Here is a characteristic tribute he paid his 'nonpareil' – his unequalled one):

> I know you are so true and loyal an Englishwoman, that you would hate those who would not stand forth in defence of our King, Laws, religion, and all which is dear to us. It is your sex that makes us go forth, and seem to tell us, 'None but the brave deserve the fair', and if we fall, we still live in the hearts of those females who are dear to us. It is your sex that rewards us, it is your sex who cherish our memories. And you, my dear honoured friend, are, believe me, the *first*, the best, of your sex. I have been the world around, and in every corner of it, and never yet saw your equal, or even one which could be put in comparison with you.

How are we to explain Nelson's profound love for Lady Hamilton? Certainly not by any overpowering physical attraction. Emma was past her prime by the time they fell in love, and steadily went downhill, physically. What then? For one thing, *Nelson needed sympathy and understanding.* Emma was a woman of passionate vitality and, in Admiral of the Fleet Lord Fisher's words, 'one mass of sympathy'. Her great merit was her warm heart. 'A woman shallow in everything but her capacity to love', says her most recent biographer, Jack Russell. Full of tenderness and marvellous sympathy, she nursed his wounded frame and fragile body after the Nile – and thereafter, for his body was always racked with increasing pain from what was then called '*tic douloureux*'. (A tic or twitch of the facial muscles accompanied by severe neuralgic pains. We now call it neuritis.) By contrast, Fanny was an iceberg – cold and unsympathetic, well-meaning but colourless, or, to put it in the least unflattering terms, a lady of calm and equable temperament, full of common sense, who seems never to have been in touch with her husband's passionate nature.

Gratitude was another component of Nelson's love for Emma. When the Admiral was in port during his anxious search for the French Fleet (before the Nile), and urgently in need of stores and provisions, which the Neapolitan authorities refused him, Emma lashed the King with her tongue and intervened with the Queen to get the fleet ready for sea – provisioned, stored, equipped. And so Nelson's heart was hers.

Most importantly, Nelson was one of those great leaders of men for whom *praise and flattery were as necessary as the air one breathes.* These Emma gave him in ample measure. Thus, after Nelson returned from the Nile, she hung the Palazzo Sessa in bunting, and blazoned his name across the façade in lights. She praised him publicly and extravagantly, and made him the centre of every occasion. 'She puffs the incense full in his face', observed Mrs St George (in 1800), 'but he receives it with pleasure and snuffs it up very cordially.'

Commented the Duchess of Devonshire long afterward: 'She fed his vanity by every art that could gratify it.' If Lady Nelson can be said to have failed her husband in any way (other than in not providing him with an heir), it was in being unable to recognize and flatter him as a great man. She was incapable of understanding the importance of his achievements. Her lack of appreciation of the value of his services to his country was a vital contributory cause of their final separation.

It never would have occurred to Emma, after the lofty deeds and stirring dramatic scenes of the Battle of St Vincent (1797), when Nelson led his men in boarding a large Spanish warship, to beg him, as Lady Nelson did, 'to leave boarding to captains'. There is, as Admiral Mahan has written, no 'thrill of response to her husband's daring in Lady Nelson's letters.'

It seems to me that without Lady Hamilton Nelson would *not* have been what he was: the greatest fighting admiral in the history of the Royal Navy. It was true what he said, or at least he ardently believed it to be true: 'Brave Emma! ... Good Emma! If there were more Emmas, there would be more Nelsons.' These were his words to Emma, after Captain Blackwood had, in September 1805, brought the news to Merton that Nelson's services might be needed very soon. Emma had ensured he would do his duty and return to sea by showing him why he must, although she could have persuaded him to stay, since he was so happy at Merton.

There are various reasons to account for the way

Emma threw herself at Nelson, *but sexual passion* (to begin with anyway) was not one of them. *First and foremost,* she was an actress – and the role of adored friend to the great hero was too good a part to miss. Always prepared to admire fame, she sat at Nelson's feet and basked in a reflected glory. Emma's life with Hamilton had been happy enough, but he was old and set in his ways; a little change and excitement was hard to resist, and seemed harmless enough when her husband himself showered Nelson with praise and rejoiced in his victorious conduct. But bad effects followed. She developed a conceit and arrogance that were totally opposite to her former character. Before she knew Nelson, she was generally liked by all the men and women of her acquaintance; with his coming, in her pride she began to make many enemies. Nelson, too, suffered moral decline from that moment. In the past his childish conceit had offended no one; but as his fame increased, he became vain in a manner that gave offence, and in his dealings with his contemporaries he was irritable and intolerant. This reputation went before him and predisposed people against him. In actual fact, the phase was transitory, and shortly before Trafalgar he regained his younger manner. Unfortunately, a great deal of harm was already done, for he had by now lost dignity in his love of adulation.

Emma never fell in love with Nelson as he did with her, for after Greville passed out of her life there was no real love left in her; but she admired Nelson *intensely*, and revelled in his fame. She firmly believed herself to be the inspiration of the great sailor. He flattered her vanity as she did his, and the couple were contented in a mutual battle of self-glorification; he even told her that she was the real victor of the Nile, and there is no doubt that she believed him!

And so ends the tale of Emma, Lady Hamilton, of her amazing rise and pathetic fall, and of her relationship with Lord Nelson – a relationship that was an important component – and, *everything considered,* a good and constructive component – in the making of England's most illustrious seaman.

———◆———

Arthur Marder's longing to write about Emma and Nelson reflected his own circumstances as an historian, for his brilliant first book *Anatomy of British Sea Power: a History of British Naval Policy in the Pre-Dreadnought Era, 1880-1905* (US edition 1940), published as *British Naval Policy, 1880-1905: The Anatomy of British Sea Power* (UK edition 1941) was making a stir on both sides of the Atlantic just as Alexander Korda's film was showing in the cinemas. Marder's book reached print at the time of Britain's greatest peril, the summer of 1940, when the nation and Empire stood alone against Hitler and the Third Reich. Norway, Poland and France had fallen to the German juggernaut and invasion of England was threatened. As the Battle of Britain was waged over the skies of England so too did *That*

Hamilton Woman bring clarity to the circumstances of the day – sea power and alliances offered Britain the only possible salvation. It was produced to meet an urgent need, with Leigh and Olivier exploited for their star value.

Originally to be called *The Enchantress*, Korda's film was released in 1941 as *Lady Hamilton*, and, in the United States, as *That Hamilton Woman*. It was an adroit attempt to enlist the help of the United States against Hitler and as such was a skillful representation of 'information', or propaganda. Hollywood was being called in to assist in the forging of an Anglo-American alliance. More than this, it portrayed one of the great love stories of the ages, with Vivien Leigh cast as Emma and Laurence Olivier as Nelson, a beautiful couple in all the raptures of love. As film critics have commented none better could have been cast for their respective parts than the glamorously illicit couple, who were at the time an adulterous pairing.

The film begins almost at the end of the tragedy. In her final lines Emma is asked by a prostitute, 'What happened then?' To this she replies, 'There is no *then* ... There is no *after*.' She had lost her lover, her home, her England, and, in debt and despair, had fled to Calais with her daughter, and Nelson's own, Horatia. Left by Nelson as a legacy to King and Country Emma and Horatia had been cast to the winds of fate, and, although the daughter does not enter the screenplay, she is a feature in the background. At one stage, on the eve of

Trafalgar, Emma proclaims that she has received the greatest gift – Nelson's own child.

Nelson is projected as the quintessential hero charged with purpose and ambition. There is more to him, as shown: he is the defender of England, not only as the gallant and successful Admiral and brilliant tactician but also a strategist of the first order. Having beaten the Danes and bringing peace with Bonaparte in the Treaty of Amiens he is shown, in a remarkable scene at the Admiralty, making plain to Lord Spencer, the First Sea Lord, and others sitting at the great table at Whitehall, that dictators are not to be trusted. A temporary peace would only be a break in the action. The dictator, in this case Bonaparte, would soon rise again and an invasion of England would be launched from across the English Channel. This was exactly the circumstance of the film's initial showing. Hitler was preparing for an invasion. The 'phoney war' was but a break in the action. Dealing with dictators was a foolish business. Here was a call to arms in time of peace, with Nelson – and England's greatest male actor, Olivier – as the messenger. In all it is a brilliant parallel to the circumstances then faced, and the viewer today, refreshed with the details of what Churchill called, 'their finest hour', cannot fail to notice the similarity of 1803 to those of 1940. Few historical films mirror the age of production, but such is the case with *That Hamilton Woman.*

As to the title of the film, twice in the dialogue we gain revelation as to who called Emma 'that Hamilton woman'. First is when Josiah Nisbet, Lady Nelson's son, and Nelson's step-son, snidely refers to Emma as the paramour of Nelson, the seductress wooing Nelson away from what should be his true connection to Josiah's mother, that is, Nelson's wife. The second comes from one of several gossiping females observing proceedings in the House of Lords when Nelson is calling forth the Peers to prepare for the greatest battle yet to come, the final challenge, derisively refers to 'that Hamilton woman'.

The film shows all the theatricality of which Emma was capable. It also shows her immense managerial capacities and organisational skills. She is the centre of attention, the commanding presence. Her ability to contend with changing circumstances, to overcome obstacles is everywhere apparent, save in the last scenes when the curtains begin to close on her life. Vivien Leigh portrays her as smart and adaptive. She lives for the present and for the hoped-for state of happiness that might come to the couple in Merton. Caught in all the swirl of events of the changing Mediterranean world, when war and revolution was on everyone's lips, not surprisingly Nelson is portrayed as the urgent Admiral with military and diplomatic obligations of the first order. It is his declining physical state, owing to loss of limb and eyesight, which brings forth Emma's close attention. And Nelson's protection of the Court at Naples, while the flames of war and revolution grow in intensity, forms the central motif of this film. Facing a continental dictator by means of naval influence, blockade, interdiction and battle, is how Nelson wages this war, and in the end, the 'Nelson touch' is implemented – a tactical action worked up in advance with Nelson's 'Band of Brothers' that gives the supreme victory of annihilation of the enemy ships – for Nelson has insisted that annihilation was the only prospect that would end Bonaparte's rise to continental, even world, domination. The film contains stirring lines that Churchill might well have written himself, but did not. When you listen to Nelson advising the Lords of the Admiralty as to the urgency of what they must do to keep command of the sea and defeat the enemy you can also turn your mind back to those dark years of the Second World War when the battle at sea had yet to be won, and when the continental dictators and their vassal states threatened the lifeblood and the future of the United Kingdom and the British Empire. It will never be known if Korda's portrayal of Emma and Nelson influenced the decision of Washington to go to war, but the odds of this are very small. It would take Pearl Harbor to do that. All the same, the themes of *That Hamilton Woman* may have helped steel the resolves of all the allies.

Marder was aware of Terrence Rattigan's play *A Bequest to the Nation*, 1970, and the film version of the same title, staring Glenda Jackson and Peter Finch, 1973. Marder thought Rattigan got it wrong. Rattigan played up the fact that Nelson, a child of the rectory and brother of a clergyman, created a great stir and attracted

England called her 'That Hamilton Bitch!'

Nelson called her 'My Dearest Emma'
– and he made her his 'Bequest to the Nation'

A HAL WALLIS Production

GLENDA JACKSON PETER FINCH

BEQUEST TO THE NATION AA

Co-starring

ANTHONY QUAYLE · MARGARET LEIGHTON · DOMINIC GUARD · NIGEL STOCK

MICHAEL JAYSTON as "Captain Hardy"

Music by Michel Legrand·Screenplay by Terence Rattigan·Directed by James Cellan Jones·Produced by Hal B.Wallis
A Universal Release·Technicolor·Distributed by Cinema International Corporation

NOW SHOWING UNIVERSAL Piccadilly Circus 930 8944

SEPARATE PERFORMANCES ALL SEATS MAY BE BOOKED IN ADVANCE
Daily 2.00 p.m., 5.00 p.m. 8.00 p.m. Sunday 4.30 p.m. 8.00 p.m. Late show Fridays & Saturdays at 11.15 p.m.

Poster for the 1973 film of Ratigan's play *Bequest to the
Nation*, released in the States as *The Nelson Affair*.

9. Sir Harry Featherstonhaugh of Uppark is depicted here as a twenty-two-year-old, five years before Emma became his mistress briefly in 1781. He turned her out on discovering she was pregnant and from him she moved to Charles Greville.

10. Emma posing in Romney's studio for the portrayal of her as The Spinstress, commissioned in 1782 by Greville, seated to the right. The scene is recreated by the Victorian artist Frank Dadd.

11. Portrait of Sir William Hamilton, British Ambassador to the Kingdom of Naples, with Vesuvius smoking in the background.

12. Emma as The Ambassadress was one of Romney's last paintings of her and was completed in September 1791 when she returned to England for her marriage to William Hamilton. Mount Vesuvius places her now firmly in Naples.

13. Emma as Cassandra, daughter of the King of Troy, who had the power of prophecy. Emma assumed a variety of characters for Romney and this aptitude was to lead to her Attitudes.

14. Emma striking some of the Attitudes for which she became famous throughout Europe. Sir William, with his knowledge of classical imagery, helped Emma design her repertoire and silent performances.

Lady H***n
Attitudes.

15. Thomas Rowlandson's provocative cartoon of Emma posing in an
Attitude, with perhaps Sir William Hamilton presenting Emma
as part of his collection. It may also allude to her earlier more
dubious work in London as a scantily clad model.

16. The village of Posillipo was the haunt of rich Neapolitans escaping the heat of the city. Villa Emma, situated on the waterfront below the road, was one of Sir William's three Naples residences and used by him and Emma for bathing.

much notoriety by leaving Frances (Lady Nelson) for Emma (Lady Hamilton). Rattigan portrays the matter as afflicting his conscience in classic Christian terms. The playwright skilfully exploited Fanny's letters to Nelson. Fanny was forgiving; she would not retaliate. This left Nelson, according to the playwright, unhinged and distraught. 'Do, my dear husband, let us live together.' So Fanny had written on 18 December 1801. 'I can never be happy until such an event takes place. I assure you again, I have but one wish in the world, to please you. Let everything be buried in oblivion, it will pass away like a dream.' Nelson did not want to retaliate; he could not. He had 'signed off' on marriage's end. She had accepted what she called 'the letter of dismissal'. However, Fanny was forgiving, and this only brought on Nelson's hate.

To close the play, Lady Nelson proffers a blessing to her successful rival, Emma. It is the noble Fanny who triumphs. The impact of forgiving love has no end, and it is Nelson who suffers, and, in the last line of the play, Lady Nelson 'hobbles her birdlike way into the darkness', walking on the thin line between love and hate. Of such emotions are the tragedies of great loves worked out. And here we leave stage and screen epics of the past wondering what next will appear. Perhaps it will be Nelson who will be portrayed as victim, a defenceless and unfortunate man of arms unprepared to deal with feminine wiles and requirements. His main calling is to the sea, and to the demands of preparing for battle and hoped-for victory. He is the great leader of men – and a director of statecraft of the first order, both as a strategist and a tactician. He is the inspiration of the 'Band of Brothers' and the originator of the ideas that brought victory at sea at the Nile, Copenhagen and Trafalgar. Females were no distraction to him: they were an essential component of his life and his hopes for the future. In a naval world dominated by men, from top to bottom, it is the female sex that brings him sustenance, care and a special brand of adoration that completes and complements everything else the martial world thunders in upon his strong but beleaguered and tortured soul. We look for the new film on Nelson, and in a world that has given us three films on William Bligh there is ample scope in the intertwining lives of Nelson, Emma, Fanny, Sir William Hamilton and that rascal Josiah Nisbet for a blockbuster.

Chapter 1 *Patroness of the Navy: the Women Behind the Fleet*

In the system of Nelson's time when interest and patronage were not only rife but also essential to advancement in rank and station, friends were essential. Navy wives made it their business to 'talent-spot' rising young midshipmen and lieutenants. From their own experiences, as navy wives and mothers, they knew the perils of upward mobility, for some had become navy widows. Many had sons in the service. Nelson had his own special patroness in Margaret Lady Parker, wife of Admiral Sir Peter Parker. Margaret had known Nelson since his days in the West Indies, and after he had been struck down by malaria contracted during the Nicaragua expedition upriver to San Juan fort, a very foolish venture, she had nursed him to health. She was of a nervous disposition and was wholeheartedly solicitous to the point of anxiety about her charge. Years later, when she knew of Nelson's further injuries and precarious health, she urged him to return home, sending letters to him directly. And by communicating by letter with Fanny (for those two became friends) Nelson's wife was able to pass on to her husband the intensity of Lady Parker's anxiety for his well-being.

Sir John Jervis, Earl St Vincent, had an aversion to naval officers marrying, especially in time of war. He was of the opinion, as reported, that newly-married officers were 'the first to run to port, and the last to come out of it.' That having been said, he was comfortable in the presence of women at sea, and treated women with kindness and civility. As eighteen-year old Betsey Wynne observed, 'he desired we should pay tribute that was due to him at our entering his Cabin, this was to kiss him which the ladies did very willingly.' Betsey was well heeled, and a political refugee: she lived in British warships for fifteen months, eventually marrying Captain Thomas Francis Fremantle of the *Inconstant*, at a ceremony in Naples in 1797. Jervis advised, or warned, Nelson that the English women of Leghorn – 'the factory' he called the English enclave – 'will find themselves very happy under your protection, and all our fair countrywomen pent up in Italy will fly to your embraces.' That was a fair assessment, and on a later occasion Nelson told Emma that he would not 'touch the pudding', loyal as he was to her.

Betsey Wynne nursed her husband and Nelson after they had been wounded at Tenerife. Both Fremantle and Nelson had been shot through the arm, and it was on this occasion that Nelson's arm was amputated. Emma and Fanny were to nurse Nelson of this wound, but it was Betsey who was there at the time doing heroic work. Wynne is important to our theme of women behind the fleet because circumstance had brought her on board a British man-of-war, the *Inconstant*, and it was on account of this that she became a naval wife. Happenstance played a big role in the forging of naval marriages. Fremantle described his bride as 'short, speaks German, Italian, French and English, plays incomparably well on the harpsichord, draws well, sings a little, and is otherwise a very good humored, sensible dolly.' Her diary of him reveals her opinions that he was 'not handsome but with fiery black eyes that are quite captivating, he is also good natured, kind, amiable, and lively, qualities that win everybody's heart.' Betsey bore him nine children – five sons, three of whom joined the Navy, and four daughters. This was the beginning of one of the remarkable naval dynasties of the nineteenth century Royal Navy. Betsey, we might note, considered Emma to be beautiful and amiable.

It is true that Nelson was easy going when it came to having women on board ships in his squadron. There were many women who lived before the mast in the *Captain*, for instance, and Nelson was indulgent when it came to requests from marine or fellow officers to accept the fact that women brought aboard, notably wives or those closely connected, should not be objected to. Having women aboard was contrary to regulations, but it was passively countenanced nonetheless and seems to have been at the discretion of the ship's captain. General de Burgh made light of it to Nelson, in teasing tone: 'Your merits are pretty generally known, your deficiencies are I believe much less so; amongst the few that have ever come to my knowledge, half-heartedness towards the fairer sex is not included.' Nelson's biographer Roger Knight, who uncovered this, makes the point that Nelson relished his independence from Fanny, by which we may infer that distance from home was beneficial in a number of ways. It was widely said at the time that a naval officer left his morals behind when he entered the Mediterranean at Gibraltar.

It was different when a ship in port was making preparations to sail. The *Vanguard*, in March 1798, had nearly three hundred women on board. Nelson determined that all were to be sent ashore, assuming the crews were paid, and the reason for this was so they could cover their debts to the females: he had resolved that not one woman would be taken to sea. All went according to plan: the crew was paid, the women disembarked, the anchor was raised, sail was made, and the ship proceeded to sea.

Women possessed an enormous benefit to the fleet, for they were great conveyors of information, and they had their own intelligence networks – letters, codes and personal gossip. Among the nobility and gentry, sharing news was a day-to-day occurrence, and often the means of social advancement. Frances Caffarena, an English

woman of the merchant community of Genoa, suppliers
of live cattle and lemons to British men-of-war, wrote
many letters to Nelson in 1796, sometimes including
translations of useful Italian documents. When Leghorn
fell to the French in June 1796 the lady in question was
almost the sole source of critical information as to local
affairs. She told Nelson about Spanish preparations by
land and sea plus other vital information. Nelson passed
on such intelligence to Gilbert Elliot and Jervis. Nelson
could do little to correct the hard times that Caffarena
faced but he valued all the information she could send.
She was a patriot and the news was of immense importance. Having secret agents and informants ashore
benefited the service, and gave further credence to
Francis Bacon's epithet 'knowledge is power'.

Women, too, were avenues to political connection in
high places. Nelson wanted Frances to accompany him
to dinner with the Earl and Countess of Spencer, and the
latter was always reluctant to bend to such importunities. She, as one of the great hostesses of the age,
would invite captains to dinner but not their wives. But
Nelson was convincing. Years later she wrote that
Nelson had made an appeal on the grounds that it would
make him the happiest man alive. He told Lavinia
Spencer that she must like Fanny. 'That she was
beautiful, accomplished, but, above all, that her angelic
tenderness to him was beyond all imagination. He told
me that his wife had dressed his wounds and that her
care alone had saved his life. In short, he pressed me to

see her, with an earnestness of which Nelson alone was capable. In these circumstances, I begged that he would bring her with him that day to dinner.' Lady Spencer held Nelson in high regard, and she was glad to have made his acquaintance: 'He is a very delightful creature & I hope I shall see him once more – tho' when I consider how little there is of him, I cannot be sanguine in such expectations.' It is clear that she did not think Nelson had long to live. She had not thought much of Nelson on first meeting some time before, regarding him as ill-mannered and a sickly creature looking much like an idiot – but ever so attractive when his marvellous mind had an opportunity to express itself, to her captivation. When Lord Spencer became First Lord of the Admiralty Nelson had a special friend at hand in Lavinia, and in the august manner that this lordship demonstrated he treated Nelson with the greatest respect and even avuncular consideration. Nelson's reputation as a great fighter had preceded him, but Lavinia's friendship engendered support in high places. On one occasion she invited Nelson to dinner because her husband wished to speak to Nelson about his new command, the *Foudroyant.*

Patronage, or interest, was essential in the advancement of naval officers. Women played an essential role as lobbyists for brothers, nephews, children and grandchildren, and for friends desiring the same for other candidates. Social standing was the top consideration. Emma, on account of her position as Nelson's mistress, lost influence at his death. She no longer had Nelson to protect her and to provide for her, and her lack of discipline was ruinous. In her new and limited state, as Margarette Lincoln explains, she could now only appeal to sentiment when seeking the advancement of a Lieutenant Jackson on board Rear-Admiral Charles Tyler's ship. 'Nelson,' she said, the 'dear Lamented Nelson', had always promised her promotion for young Jackson, and now should the Admiral be passing near Richmond she suggested that he should call on her and reminisce of times past. In Emma, Britannia's glory began to fade quickly, and she was cast on stormy seas and shores, humiliated and ridiculed. Long gone were the days and even the memories of having sailed with Nelson in the Mediterranean, under his complete protection and that of his fleet.

Some examples of women in British naval annals in more modern times show the continuing power of the distaff side in the exercise of sea power. Rear-Admiral the Hon Joseph Denman, who acquired fame from his close-in actions against the slave pens of the West African coast, where the slaves were kept before being sent out in the surf boats to the waiting slave ships, took his wife out to the distant Pacific Station in the 1860s when he was Commander-in-Chief. Another, Captain (later Admiral) George Henry Richards, the famous surveyor, had his wife with him on the same station, and their children who were born during his tour of duty were given local names. Many naval officers 'on station' married colonial women. Such particulars as these suggest the importance of women afloat in the nineteenth-century navy and the permissiveness of the Admiralty allowing such arrangements afloat.

In the early twentieth century females took on powerful positions when their husbands were at, or near, top levels of command. For instance, Lady Jellicoe, wife of Admiral Sir John Jellicoe, Commander of the Grand Fleet at Jutland, 31 May–1 June 1916) and later First Sea Lord, carefully guarded his reputation, as the following recounts. Admiral Sir David Beatty, who commanded the Battle Cruiser force in the same battle, was married to the divorcee Edith (*nee* Field) Tree (Beatty fixed this arrangement), daughter of the Chicago millionaire store magnate, Marshall Fields. She brought a fortune into an otherwise impoverished noble family, sufficient to have her own yacht *Sheelah* at anchor not far from where her husband's ship, the battle cruiser *Lion*, lay in the Firth of Forth. Beatty became a critic of Jellicoe's leadership and actions at Jutland. A great controversy ensued in what is known as 'the Jutland scandal', with Beatty, then First Sea Lord, fudging the official record about what transpired at Jutland. Montagues and Capulets abounded. Jutland was a battle without end. The controversy even continued after death, as this anecdote tells. Jellicoe died in 1935 and was buried near Nelson in the crypt at St Paul's. Lady Jellicoe was furious when she learned that Beatty was to be buried beside her husband. She made a passionate appeal to the Dean and Chapter and then the Admiralty that this must not happen. She received the disheartening reply that the decision was one of state, the crypt being a national shrine. She replied in brusque fashion to Lord Chatfield, then First Sea Lord: 'I do appreciate the fact you and the Admiralty are not to blame about St Paul's. Strange that the Church instead of giving you Peace of Mind should destroy it.' Chatfield's son Ernle, the 2nd Baron, told historian Arthur Marder that his father always thought it was the wives who had exacerbated the Jellicoe-Beatty dispute over Jutland.

Declining mental health under the stress of war and wartime led the women behind the fleet into all sorts of difficulties and took their men into different channels rather than bringing their ships and fleets safely into harbour. The wandering Lady Beatty was a neurotically sick wife, and the Earl was endlessly solicitous in trying to end her worry and her misery. For consolation and friendship he took up with the wife of a fellow naval officer, the adorable and adoring Eugenie Godfrey-Fausset. This was perhaps the naval romance of the twentieth century, and similarly tortuous to that of Emma and Nelson, but passed without much gossip or social spiking. Some day more will be known about Edith and Eugenie – and from Beatty's perspective the former provided agony and the latter ecstasy. Some marriages provide neither. He was patiently devoted to his wife, wrote Geoffrey Bennett, a retired naval officer, in his *Battle of Jutland*, and bore this all without complaint. 'There are aspects of Nelson's life which are open to sharper criticism, but no one questions his right to look down on the heart of London from the summit of a column in Trafalgar Square.'

In many cases navy wives wore more gold braid than their husbands. They glorified the history of the Navy, and they gloried in its greatness. After all, they played their share in its success – as wives, mothers and keepers of the flame. One of them, Lady Marjorie Duff, widow of Admiral Sir Alexander Duff (who had instituted convoys in April 1917 on a trial basis), insisted that the historian Arthur Marder meet all sorts of other naval widows and thereby have the chance to consult the golden treasures to be found in the naval papers kept in their private hands. She made the introductions; Marder did the rest. Widows wanted their husbands included in the historical record. They also wanted the full story of Britain's sea battles to be known, especially in an age when other services were receiving ever more (and, some thought, unwarranted) attention. And let us not leave out mothers. David Beatty's mother had a full size portrait of Nelson painted for her son, and he kept it on exhibit in the captain's room of the battlecruiser *Lion*.

The diplomatic influence of women 'on station' was out of all proportion to their few numbers. Admiral Sir Frederick Dreyer, C-in-C Far East, had his wife Una, Lady Dreyer with him on various visits to Japan. Although we do not know the impact this made on the

Japanese we do know that the social relations with the United States Ambassador to Japan and his wife were important in helping the Dreyers gain a better understanding of the Japanese and their political system. Even to the days of the last First Sea Lord the power of women remained influential. Earl Mountbatten of Burma's wife, Edwina, bought money and social influence to the marriage. She was closely connected to Nehru when her husband was Viceroy of India and may have influenced the course of Indian independence or later politics. As for the Earl, he later confessed that for most of his life and that of his wife they had spent much time in and out of the beds of other people.

Finally, there is the sad business of Lord Prince Louis Mountbatten, the German born Admiral of the Fleet who was one of the Navy's greatest sailors and administrators. A campaign of persecution began with Lord Charles Beresford from the time he obtained senior responsibility, about 1907, and aided by journalists and cruel and bigoted naval officers and their wives the Prince was driven from his post as First Sea Lord in November 1914, to be replaced by Sir John Fisher. Fisher, we might note in passing and conclusion, lived his later life far from his loving wife. Instead, he took up a close sexual liaison with an American, the Duchess of Hamilton, wife of a naval officer. The husband was an invalid and a friend of Jacky's (Fisher). In later years, Admiral Lord Fisher was fond of the thought that he, too, like Nelson, had his own adoring Lady Hamilton. We leave this theme now, a little sadly, for there is much more to be written about 'the women behind the fleet'. We know in Fanny Nisbet and Emma, Lady Hamilton Horatio Nelson had two powerful and devoted women to contend with, and it will always be a matter of fascinating conjecture as to what further chapters would have been written had Nelson not met immortality at the Battle of Trafalgar.

Chapter 2 *Emma Meets Hamilton*

Emma met her future husband, Sir William Hamilton, in London in 1784. She was then attached to Sir William's nephew, the Hon Charles Greville, who contrary to everything Emma expected, and perhaps even hoped for, had run up sizeable debts that he could not cover. Sir William, well connected in diplomatic and government circles, was an antiquarian, fascinated by Greek and Roman antiquities. His love of Greek and Roman history and letters had the wonderful influence of giving Emma examples to imitate and interpret in her Attitudes, then a prevailing entertainment in select, higher circles. He was well connected in Georgian England as a purveyor of treasures from Naples and the Mediterranean generally. In London, Sir William knew that George Romney, the portrait painter, had executed a beautiful portrait of Emma.

Truth to tell he saw Emma then as a vehicle or means of bringing to life the classical age. Her beauty alone and her grace spelled the sort of perfection that Sir William could see for his future requirements. Here was art imitating life, and also the opposite. Sir William knew Emma's darker past – how she had been kept by Sir Harry Featherstonhaugh at Uppark, a truly wonderful destination for extravagant parties of the upper classes. Perhaps, too, he knew that she had given birth to a daughter, 'Little Emma', who had been placed in care elsewhere. Sir William also knew of Emma's even earlier past, that of her teenage years, when she had been in household service, then employed in Dr Graham's Temple of Health, in the Adelphi, an electricity-charged establishment dedicated to sexual arousal and the promotion of pregnancy. He knew of her as an actress and also, most likely, as a prostitute.

All of these features of Emma's story, and perhaps even those of her childhood, Sir William was prepared to set aside: to him Emma was seen as daily growing in health and beauty as well as value, and although it is tempting to conceive that he saw her as an object that would favour his own designs of collecting and selling antiques of the classical age, it is certain that he was not without many personal affinities to Emma and fell in love with her. She, too, fell in love with Sir William. In September 1791 they were married in St George's Church, Hanover Square, London.

On the day of her marriage, on her return from church, Romney completed *The Ambassadress*, in which she wears one of her favourite blue hats, with Vesuvius behind her. Her famed Attitudes led to many a subject

17. King Ferdinand IV, whose armies were routed after encouragement by Nelson to attack Rome in 1798, was forced to flee from Naples to Palermo. Emma was present on board Nelson's ship during the stormy crossing to Sicily.

18. Maria Carolina, Queen of Naples and Sicily was the sister of Marie Antoinette. She and Emma became close friends and the latter acquired significant influence at the Neapolitan Court.

19. A perspective view of Naples *c*1795. The Castello Nuovo at
Naples, the city residence of Ferdinand IV and Maria Caroline
is on the waterfront in the centre.

20. Emma as a Bacchante, painted in 1792 by the fashionable
French portraitist Louise-Elizabeth Vigée Le Brun who
emigrated to Italy after the French Revolution. In her memoirs
she lays stress on Emma's great beauty and chestnut hair.

21. In this portrayal of Nelson by Lemuel Abbott he wears on his hat the diamond chelengk sent him by the Sultan of the Ottoman Empire in gratitude for saving Egypt (an Ottoman province) from Napoleon.

22. Fanny Nelson, painted during perhaps the
happiest period of her marriage, after devotedly
nursing Nelson back to health in 1797.
By the time she next saw him, in 1800,
he and Emma had become lovers.

23. The French fleet, at anchor in Aboukir Bay, was destroyed by Nelson at the Battle of the Nile, the first of his three great victories, and he returned to Naples a hero. French naval power in the Mediterranean had been eliminated, literally overnight, and the capture or destruction of eleven out of thirteen French ships of the line was an unprecedented feat of naval annihilation.

24. Nelson soon became a household name throughout Europe and this cartoon by Gillray presents an unambiguous celebration of the victory and depicts the hero thrashing the tricoloured revolutionary crocodiles with a club of 'British Oak'. In the distance is reference to the explosion of *L'Orient*, the French flagship.

25. *Vanguard* arriving back at Naples on 22 September 1798 after the victory at the Battle of the Nile. Emma and Nelson's liaison began during the festivities at Naples that followed his victory.

for a picture – as Circe, for example, or Cleopatra or her favourite, Medea. The foremost painter in Naples, Angelica Kauffmann, represented Emma as the Comic Muse. Goethe, observing Emma, wrote that the spectator 'sees what thousands of artists would have liked to express, realised before him in movements and surprising transformations – one pose follows another without a break. She knows how to arrange the folds of her veil to match each mood, and has a hundred ways of turning it into a headdress.' Romney painted her countless times, once as *The Seamstress* and another *Emma at Prayer*. Still another, *The Spinstress*, was commissioned by Greville, himself a collector; it is regarded as Romney's finest work. Rowlandson drew the cartoon of Emma posed among marble statues, working in Dr Graham's Temple. Another nude representation exists, *From the Nude*, probably painted by Romney, and once in the possession of Captain John Peyton, one of Nelson's Band of Brothers. It is small wonder that the Captain, who knew Fanny and Nelson well, wanted to possess a naked portrait of the woman who was his Admiral's mistress.

Greville had liquidated his debts by sending Emma to Naples, and Sir William had accepted this as a bargain. He solved his nephew's problem and acquired the beauty of the age. This turn of events Emma took by surprise but she accepted the new state of affairs. She became a powerful force at the Court in Naples. She was in her element, and she was far from the wagging tongues of England. This suited her perfectly. Naples was then managed by Sir John Acton, the Prime Minister, who built up the naval and military capacities of the Kingdom of the Two Sicilies. Emma was that sort of individual who filled every social vacuum; she was larger than life, as one might say. She was not a person to rest on her laurels and merely be consort to Sir William, the British Ambassador. No, as Emma, Lady Hamilton she had her own roles to fill in the enhancing of the alliance that existed between Great Britain and the Kingdom of the Two Sicilies. Bonaparte was the rising threat, but the revolutionary fervour then sweeping though the old empires of Europe at that time affected Naples. Emma was on the side of the King and Queen, Ferdinand IV and Maria Carolina. For five years between the time she first met Nelson and his return, when they fell in love, she played the important roles as courtier and fixer, political aide and diplomatic advisor. Sir William Hamilton, and the British ministry, had an essential ally in Emma.

Sir William gave his wife every advantage and encouragement. Greville had promised that she would have French and Italian lessons, and this was arranged. Sir William encouraged her performances of the Attitudes and facilitated her abilities as an opera singer. Her talents were without number. She was the most remarkable and beautiful woman of the age. She attracted adoration, and deserved it. Hers is a Pygmalion story, for sometimes when she spoke she disclosed her past. She was the daughter of a blacksmith, had been born near Liverpool, and had in her company the wonderful Mary, Mrs Cadogan, her devoted mother and her tender and encouraging confidant.

But Emma lacked one thing: true love. Men would fall at her feet, as they had done in the past. None, however, had filled her greatest need. Nelson came into her life as Emma's man of destiny. He, too, was in search of life's greatest need.

Chapter 3 *Emma Meets Nelson*

O n 12 September 1793, Nelson, in his favourite ship, the two-decker *Agamemnon*, mounting 64 guns, cast anchor in Palermo, the harbour of Naples, the second capital of the King and Queen of Naples and Sicily (otherwise, the Two Sicilies). He had become her Captain when war had broken out with France once again. He had been unemployed for four years, and feared that Admiralty opposition kept him away from a sea command. Many of the ship's complement were Norfolk men, and it was a happy and efficient ship.

Nelson had come to Naples to seek reinforcements for Toulon, and in making his appeal to the British minister plenipotentiary, Sir William Hamilton (who was to become one of his great friends) he met with much support. Sir William promised six thousand troops to sail under the convoy of the *Agamemnon*. They were taken immediately to Toulon, and Nelson had acted quickly in all of this and the Kingdom of the Two Sicilies and England were joined in common cause.

It was on this same day, 12 September 1783, that Nelson met the already famous Emma, Lady Hamilton, and although there was no immediate social or sexual attraction disclosed by Nelson the attractiveness of this thirty-year-old did not fail to gain his attention. He reported to Fanny: 'Lady Hamilton has been wonderfully kind and good to Josiah [his step-son]. She is a young woman of amiable manners, who does honour to the station to which she is raised.' It did not escape notice, therefore, that Emma had risen beyond her previous station.

Nelson went to Naples, but did not go ashore. Instead, he wrote to Emma saying that as soon as he fought the French fleet he would do the honour of paying his respects to her at Naples 'and I hope to be congratulated on a victory'. That brought this response: 'I will not say how glad I shall be to see you. Indeed I cannot describe to you my feelings of your being so near us.' She sent a letter from the Queen demanding that Nelson 'kiss it and send it back'.

Nelson and his ships then combed the eastern Mediterranean and eventually found the French fleet anchored at Aboukir Bay, an approach to the Nile delta. 'Before this time tomorrow,' he exclaimed, 'I shall have gained a peerage, or Westminster Abbey.' Yes, glory or death! Nelson had made clear to his captains his intentions and his designs. The action commenced at sunset on 1 August 1798, and was fought with celerity and vigour unsurpassed in the history of naval combat to that time. During the heat of the attack Nelson received a severe head injury. A flying fragment that sliced open his head caused Nelson's wound, and a flap of skin fell over his eye temporarily blinding him. 'I am killed. Remember me to my wife', he told Captain Sir Edward Berry. It was a victory of immense importance, Nelson's first of three great triumphs. Eleven of thirteen French battleships were captured or destroyed. Napoleon had been denied Egypt and points leading to India. Nelson's fame spread throughout Europe, and took on a new lustre in England and, not least, at the Admiralty.

Emma learned of the victory when two naval officers arrived in Naples, with urgent dispatches from Nelson to the Admiralty. They gave Sir William a letter from Nelson proclaiming the merits and effects of the battle: 'Almighty God has given me the happy instrument in destroying the Enemy's Fleet, which I hope will be a blessing to Europe.' Emma rushed to tell the Queen the news, then, in a carriage, paraded the two officers through the streets to shouts of *'Viva Nelson'*. The glorification, Neapolitan style, had begun. For the festive occasion to follow, Emma dressed herself in a shawl of blue with gold anchors all over. 'My ear-rings are Nelson's anchors', she wrote to Nelson in expectation of seeing him at the first possible moment, 'in short, we are be-Nelsoned all over.'

When Nelson returned, Emma greeted him with, 'O God! Is it possible?' She fell into a swoon. The great and generous celebrations for the victor of the Nile were also proclaiming freedom from French domination, something premature in fact. Nelson was the hero of the hour, and Naples the perfect civic backdrop. The allure of the city, the reassurance of fame, and the newly-realised glories of Emma began to play on him. These were heady hours and days for the hero of the Nile. At first Nelson thought Naples 'No place for a simple sailor', but the flagship needed repairs, delaying his departure by four days. 'The Conqueror has become the Conquered', he later told Emma.

Emma had written to Fanny to tell her of Nelson's arrival and reception by their Sicilian Majesties and to pass on the Queen's congratulations and compliments. She wrote again, on 2 December, that Nelson was adored and regarded as deliverer of the country. He had recovered from his poor state. His wound was 'quite well'. 'Sir William and herself,' Emma said, 'were ever so happy of seeing our dear, respectable, brave friend return here with so much honour to himself and glory to his country.' She added two further matters of importance. First, that Josiah had improved in many respects and would make a fine officer: 'I love him much and although we quarrel sometimes, he loves me and does as I would have him.' And second, that Sir William was in a rage at the news that Nelson had not been made a viscount, only a baron. Sir William put it this way, poignantly: 'For sure this great and glorious action, greater than any other, ought to have been recompensed more. Hang them I say.'

'All confess him to be their saviour and deliverer', was the way Sir William described Nelson to Earl St Vincent, the prominent Admiral who directed naval affairs. Nelson had earned fame throughout Europe. The Battle of the Nile had made him the invincible one, the saviour of British interests. 'In short no words can express what is felt here [in Naples], and the consequences of this most important and well timed action are incalculable.' The dockyards made everything ready for Nelson's ships; nothing was denied. Nelson worried that St Vincent may have felt that Nelson was coming too near him in reputation, and he wrote to Fanny to that effect. He need not have feared this, for St Vincent was one of his champions.

So was Sir William Hamilton. When ashore Nelson stayed in the residence of Sir William and Emma, Lady Hamilton. The British Ambassador, not far off his seventieth birthday, was a collector of antiquities, 'the volcano lover' Susan Sontag calls him. It was not that he was a dilettante but he had an air of distraction about him. All the same, he was a grand host at his residence Palazzo Sessa, with its grand view of the smouldering volcano and all its ancient associations. Hamilton's passion was collecting, which benefitted the British nation on the one hand, and his pocket on the other. Sir William was a fellow who embraced visitors, made them welcome – and so it was with Nelson. He had every intention of keeping Emma happy and content, pleased as he was that she had great influence at the Court of the Kingdom of Naples and Sicily, in particular with the powerful queen, Maria Carolina, daughter of Maria Theresa of Austria, sister of the late Marie Antoinette. Emma was her closest friend.

The British government had formed a protective shield around the Kingdom of the Two Sicilies, and Nelson and his squadron were its guardians. If the King and Queen of Naples were to survive they must seek shelter in Sicily. Nelson put in place a plan, and with the resourceful Emma guiding the royal personages through subterranean passages they reached the *Vanguard*. Sir William and Mrs. Cadogan, plus others, were safely aboard by midnight 21 December. A terrible storm delayed their progress towards Palermo, but the party had escaped the pro-French mob at Naples. The world seemed upside down, and all was in chaos, all in danger. Sir William was miserable, on account of the loss of many of his antiquities that went down with the *Colossus*. It was time for him to say goodbye to Naples and return home to a comfortable retirement. He took comfort in his friendship with Nelson. Emma's actions brought acclaim in the pages of *The Times* (28 January 1799): 'We are informed from a very respectable authority that the Queen owed much to the address of Lady Hamilton, who assisted in her getting away.' The French entered Naples and set up a republic. The British returned with their ships and blockaded the port and, aided by some irregulars, liberated Naples. Nelson fared poorly, for he was complicit in the heavy-handed reprisals that were part of the re-occupation and the calling to account those who had been complicit in the fall of the Government in the first place. There were atrocities and Emma was not free from charges that she had played her part in the barbarities. We do not know the details, but the charges are damning.

1799 was a year of extraordinary difficulties for the hero of the Nile. He was fatigued and far from home. He longed for rest and repose though was conflicted understandably by his tremendously strong concept of duty. 'I want rest,' he confided to a fellow naval officer, and he began to exercise his command from ashore, the first and only time in his career he did so. He was chafing under Admiral Lord Keith's command, and in private letters to Emma was scathing in his attack on his superior. And there was more. Colin White, collector of his recently discovered letters, says Nelson was in early 1800 tortured by guilt on account of his amiable and dangerous liaison with Emma. But he had made up his mind. There was no turning back.

On 29 January 1800, six days from Leghorn on his most recent mission, and steering for Palermo, Nelson wrote to Emma in fullest confidence and undoubted transparency as to his emotions and anxieties. He began by saying that he was separated from all he held dear in the world. The call of country – that is, duty – had brought much loitering, standing around waiting for action that never seemed to come. But separation from Emma, he said, was founded on 'the truest principles of honour', and he regretted that he was also pulled away from her by obligation of rigid marital rules. He assured Emma that they were drawn together by real love, and in words of intensity wrote, 'Continue only to love your faithful Nelson as he loves his Emma.' Emma was his guide, he said: 'Let me find all my fond heart hopes and wishes with the risk of my life.'

The next day, the 30th, he wrote once again in this familiar strain. He was still far away from Palermo and beloved Emma, and could neither eat nor sleep for thinking of his dearest love. A gale had sent his ship farther from Emma's embrace, and night had only brought visions. He recounted a dream in which she had appeared, setting aside all distress, and whispered to him, 'I love nothing but you my Nelson. I kissed you fervently and we enjoy'd the height of love.' Every sea mile closed between his ship and Palermo eased his mind, and fair wind made him better thinking of the tender and explosive hours in her arms, in her bed. In those long and desperate days at sea it was the promise of reassuring love that kept him to his task. His sense of duty rested on his emotional ties to his dear Emma.

At the height of his martial powers, England's naval hero exhibited all the emotional frailties of one under stress at the supreme moment. He was the glorious victor of the Nile, and had denied Bonaparte his eastern imperial visions. But Nelson expressed every human foible when distant from Emma sailing the storm-tossed Mediterranean. His mind was racing, racing ahead in anticipation of warm nights ashore in loving arms. He did not see duty and love in conflict. He saw them intertwined. He gives no indication that destiny had any role to play. Nor does he indicate that he and Emma had been thrown together by circumstance. No, this was true love raised to the highest level. The great hero needed, desperately, a great lover – the complete emotional partner who could also bring him to the highest sexual revelations, a not inconsiderable achievement considering his battered and emaciated body, his loss of limb and of sight in one eye, a bad head wound, and, not to be forgotten, pain from a hernia.

And what of Emma? Her letters to Nelson do not survive. We can imagine however that no matter how strongly she loved Sir William – and indeed she did love him – she loved Nelson without reservation. Perhaps for the first time in her adventurous life she was in command of her own situation. Nelson had given her that freedom to love unreservedly. Yes, there were legal difficulties and obligations, gossips to contend with and hurtful comments abounding at home and abroad. Leaving aside the powerful attraction of a great naval hero (undeniable to Emma, for she, too, quested for fame) she had found in the needy and attentive Nelson her complete requirement in love and devotion. Here was a glorious love fully expressed and fully achieved. It ranks among the great love stories because it rests on the essence of human love caught up in the foibles and heady circumstances of the times. Say what you will, this was no casual affair: this was the perfection of human emotions of longing and desire, the union of spirits.

Two years after the Battle of the Nile Jervis urged Emma to keep an eye on Nelson and not let him wander with the fair sex. 'Pray do not let your fascinating Neapolitan dames approach too near him, for he is made of flesh & blood & cannot resist their temptation.' Jervis knew his man. But Nelson has reassured Emma, in that same revealing letter that began on 29 January 1800, 'I never touch even pudding you know the reason. No I would starve sooner. My only hope is to find you have equally kept your promises to me, for I never made you a Promise that I did not as strictly keep as if made in the presence of heaven.'

Chapter 4 *Emma Meets Fanny*

On 6 November 1800 the Admiral stepped ashore at Yarmouth to a tumultuous local welcome. In his party were Sir William Hamilton and Lady Hamilton, Mrs Cadogan and Cornelia Knight – friends all. The hero of the Battle of the Nile had returned to his native soil. His first action was to send a letter to the Admiralty saying that his health had been unreservedly re-established and that he wished to return to active service immediately.

However, from that moment on the trouble began. Everywhere Nelson met adulation. Only his wife played the role of the cautious admirer, for her son Josiah, the young naval officer, had, as Julia Frankau puts it, 'supplied her with sufficient information to poison her mind, and the accounts of the receptions at the various foreign Courts inflamed it further.' As the same author puts it, 'She had had no part in Nelson's triumphs, no share in his glory; that lot being reserved for Lady Hamilton. Even if her affection for her husband had been greater than there is reason to suppose was the case, her forbearance would have been strained beyond the point of endurance at the publicity of the affront now put upon her by his conduct towards another woman.' His infatuation was patent to the world, and therein lay the essence of the matter.

In advance of his arrival, Nelson had sent Fanny a note saying that he and his party would call at Roundwood, Rushmere, Ipswich, the small country house he and Fanny had acquired, and a location on the route to London. Fanny never received the note, for she had gone to London to await Nelson there. Nelson faced disappointment and arrived to an empty dinner table. Three days later, on 9 November, Nelson and the Hamiltons reached London, and took suites in Nerot's Hotel, King Street, St James's, one of Sir William's favourites. Fanny knew from newspaper reports all about the goings-on of her husband and Emma. Nelson played his hand coolly, assuming he could go free of censure. Emma was then pregnant by Nelson, and her size could not have escaped Fanny's inquiring and censorious eyes. Emma was bright, on her best behaviour, and Sir William, the skilled Ambassador, eased that first meeting. But Fanny could clearly see the closeness and familiarity of the *tria juncta in uno* (as Sir William called them).

On the Monday, Nelson made his appearance at the Admiralty, where he called on that grandee Lord Spencer, the First Lord St Vincent, the senior Admiral in charge of naval operations. Spencer wanted Nelson at sea, as Second-in-Command for a Baltic expedition. That suited Nelson nicely, for not only was life simpler at sea than on land but Nelson had debts to settle, and his expenses were rising quickly. Prize money would ease the matter. Sir William depended on Nelson's credit, and meeting Emma's lavish expenditures had no limits. Nelson, the centre of all attention, received a special sword from the City of London, and he was mobbed at his arrival and departure. The opposite was true at Court. The King gave Nelson rather a cold shoulder at a levee, preferring to talk to a general. Perhaps the King disapproved of Nelson wearing foreign decorations, or perhaps His Majesty was suffering from a bout of what has been described as his madness (actually porphyria). There is a third possibility. Perhaps he objected to Nelson's dangerous liaison with Emma and Sir William Hamilton. In any event, that evening Nelson's rage at his ill-treatment by the monarch was vented on the unfortunate Fanny as they dined with the Spencers. On that occasion, Fanny prepared some walnuts for Nelson to eat only to find them being pushed aside roughly, and a glass damaged in the process. When the ladies retired, Fanny unburdened herself and told the sympathetic Lavinia, Countess Spencer, of her difficulties. There was a chill in the air, and all sensed it.

For the next few days the social whirl of London consumed these persons, and at the theatre the valiant conqueror of the Nile, or Aboukir, was cheered. Day

26. The poster for the 1941 Korda film, *That Hamilton Woman*, staring Vivien Leigh and Laurence Olivier. It is said that Churchill helped write some of the big speeches and contributed the famous line, 'You can't make peace with dictators.'

27. A still of Vivien Leigh as Emma in *That Hamilton Woman*. The difficult subject of adultery in the 1940s was to some extent bypassed by a rather inaccurate portrayal of Emma embracing domesticity.

Lord NELSON'S _Reception at_ FONTHILL.

28. After their return to England, Emma, Nelson and Hamilton
spent the Christmas of 1800 at Fonthill Abbey, the home
of William Beckford, novelist, collector and kinsman
of Sir William. Fanny Nelson was left in London,
along with her father.

29. Rowlandson's acerbic pen alludes to Emma and Nelson's affair in the embracing couple, ogled at by an outraged ancient, easily identified as Hamilton, with a cuckold's horns at his feet. The Egyptian artefacts remind the viewer of the Battle of the Nile.

30. Poor Hamilton is further mocked in this Gillray cartoon which shows him examining antiquites while hanging in the background, behind cuckold's horns, is a topless Cleopatra with gin bottle (Emma), Mark Antony in naval uniform, an erupting Vesuvius and Claudius under more cuckold's horns.

31. The most blatant sexual satire is on display in Isaac Cruikshank's 1800 cartoon in which Nelson replies to Emma's complaint that 'the old man's pipe is always out,' with 'I'll give you such a smoke. I'll pour a whole broadside into you.'

32. Horatia, born in January 1801, and the only child of
Emma and Nelson, had to be kept a secret as long as Sir
William was alive. Only just before Trafalgar did Nelson
openly admit to her parentage. Emma never did so.

33. This was Nelson's favourite portrait of Emma and hung in his cabin on *Victory*. He is said to have referred to it as his 'guardian angel'. It depicts her wearing the Maltese Cross, awarded for her help securing supplies to Malta during the French occupation of 1798.

after day the acclaim continued. Baron Nelson of the Nile and Burnham Thorpe took his place in the House of Lords on 20 November, to much adulation.

But Emma could never be welcomed at Court, even as a representative of the Queen of the Two Sicilies, for her reputation had preceded her. She never failed to pay attention to Sir William, always solicitous.

All the same, scuttlebutt was rife and scandalous talk common, and it was in these circumstances that the London scene took away from her one of her closest associates, Cornelia Knight, who abandoned her on the strength of advice from Sir Thomas Troubridge, a rising admiral. The flattering Cornelia had no principles in regards to friendship, and in this case friendship was betrayed, and Nelson, when informed of this, referred to her as 'that b____ Miss Knight'. The social whirl continued in London, the Hamiltons and the Nelsons often at the theatre together – Fanny sitting on one side of the Admiral, Emma on the other. This tight circle betrayed the deepest emotions, soon to break forth and consume the principals.

No two persons could be as different as Emma and Fanny. The one was flamboyant and by nature an extrovert, beautiful and voluptuous; her rival was reserved and exact in manner, pretty and rigidly upright. Both were of strong character. They were opposites in social background, too: Emma, raised from the working classes; Fanny, from the planter class of the West Indies. They spoke in different dialects, indicative of social status, blood and breeding. And all eyes were on them.

The *Morning Herald* of 13 November 1800 gave its readership an account of Emma, as seen at the theatre:

Lady Hamilton – the lady of Sir William Hamilton, KB, who with her husband has lately accompanied Lord Nelson to England being variously spoken of as to her personal charms, a short sketch of her exterior may be acceptable to many of our readers. Her ladyship is in her 35th year: rather taller than the common height; still displaying a superior graceful animation of figure, now a little on the wane from too great a propensity to the *embonpoint*. Her attitudinarian graces, so varying in their style and captivating in their effect, are declining also under this unfortunate personal extension [of pregnancy]. Her teeth are lovely, and her hair is of the darkest brown, immensely thick and trails to the ground. Her eyes are black and possess the most fascinating attraction, but her nose is rather too short for the Grecian contour of her face, which notwithstanding is singularly expressive and her conversaziones, if not solid and argumentative, are at least sprightly and unceasing. Such after ransacking Herculaneum and Pompeii for thirty-eight years is the chief curiosity with which that celebrated antiquarian Sir William Hamilton has returned to his native country.

On 19 November 1800 the same journal described Fanny in comparison with her rival:

Lady Nelson appeared in white with a violet satin head-dress and a small white feather. Her ladyship's person is of a very pleasing description: her features are handsome and exceedingly interesting, and her general appearance is at once prepossessing and elegant. Lady Hamilton is rather *embonpoint* but her person is nevertheless highly graceful and her face extremely pretty. She wore a blue satin gown and head-dress with a fine plume of feathers.

A few nights later they were all at Drury Lane for a performance of 'Pizarro', the conqueror of Peru. It was a packed house – 'a most splendid assemblage of beauty and fashion'. Once again Lord and Lady Nelson and Sir William and Lady Hamilton formed the brilliant circle, and were the subject of attention. As the same paper reported on 25 November 1800:

His Lordship on his entrance was received with the most flattering testimonials of public regard; and *Rule Britannia*, with an additional verse in favour of the gallant hero of the Nile, was sung amidst the universal plaudits of the admiring crowd. After the play, Charles Dibdin's song *The Lass that Loved the Sailor*, both Nelson's and the Navy's favourite, was sung in character by the popular tenor of the day Charles Dignum and deservedly encored; and every opportunity was eagerly seized by the audience to evince the high estimation in which they held the valiant conqueror of Aboukir. The heat, owing to the crowd, was so great that towards the end of the third act Lady Hamilton fainted away, and was obliged to be carried out of her box. Her Ladyship however soon became sufficiently recovered to resume her seat, and to the great satisfaction of all present remained in the box during the rest of the performance. We understand she has for some days been in an indifferent state of health.

And then came a tour (Fanny excluded) to Salisbury, where Nelson received the Freedom of the City, followed by a visit to William Beckford's fabulous Fonthill to the welcome of *Rule Britannia* and a round of merriment and celebration. There, at a performance, Emma's fashion-setting Attitudes brought acclaim.

On 1 January Nelson was promoted Vice-Admiral of the Blue, and now only two steps lay to that of full admiral. By now it was known that he would soon go to sea.

It was a time of great anguish for the Admiral. He was consumed by jealousy, afraid that Emma would be made into a sexual victim by the propositions of Sir William to the importunate Prince of Wales. Nelson knew that the Prince had amorous designs on Emma, and Nelson knew that Sir William Hamilton was pressing to entertain the Prince with Emma present. Against Nelson's objection and his inflamed jealousy at the thought of Emma giving in to the Prince's advances, the dinner and evening went ahead. During these days Emma suffered at least one migraine headache, and

Nelson saw her as vulnerable – a potential victim. He was powerless to intervene. He yearned for a means of escape with her, but duty, his most powerful persuader, called.

On 1 March Nelson said his goodbyes to Emma. She was then two weeks short of delivering twins, Horatia and the other child stillborn. He wrote tenderly to Emma baring all:

> Now my dear wife, for such you are in my eyes and in the face of Heaven, I can give full scope to my feelings. You know, my dearest Emma, that there is nothing in this world that I would not do for us to live together, and to have our dear little child with us. I firmly believe that this campaign will give us peace, and then we will set off for Bronte. In twelve hours we shall be across the water and freed from all the nonsense of his [Sir William's] friends, or rather pretended ones. Nothing but an event happening to him could prevent my going, and I am sure you will think so, for unless all matters accord it would bring a hundred of tongues and slanderous reports if I separated from her [Lady Nelson] (which I would do with pleasure the moment we can be united. I want to see her no more), therefore we must manage till we can quit this country or your uncle [Sir William] dies.

Nelson was due to sail, and he predicted a victorious return. He imagined how Emma would feel seeing her

Nelson now perhaps with a little more fame, 'her own dear loving Nelson'. He continued,

> You, my beloved Emma, and my country, are the two dearest objects of my fond heart – a heart susceptible and true. Only place confidence in me and you never shall be disappointed ... What must be my sensations at the idea of sleeping with you! It sets me on fire, even the thoughts, much more would the reality. I am sure my love and desires are all to you, and if any woman naked were to come to me, even as I am this moment thinking of you, I hope it might rot off if I would touch her even with my hand. No, my heart, person, and mind is in perfect union of love towards my own dear, beloved Emma – the real bosom friend of her, all hers, all Emmas...

His departure from Fanny was equally difficult. She wanted reconciliation, and she never discarded her love for her husband. She was well aware of his slights and equally aware of his devotion to Emma. Then came the break. William Haslewood, Nelson's solicitor, recounts the story. Apparently Fanny became alarmed when Nelson referred again to 'dear Lady Hamilton'. Fanny rose from her chair. She strongly exclaimed: 'I am sick of hearing of dear Lady Hamilton, and am resolved that you shall give up either her or me.' In other words, Fanny, perhaps in exasperation, had given Nelson the ultimatum – her or me, and that eventually she 'muttered something about her mind being made up ...

and shortly afterwards drove from the house. They never lived together again.' Nelson wrote to Fanny twice en route to his ship, the *San Josef*, and there he hoisted his flag. Nelson sent his usual carping letters to Fanny about insufficient consideration of the material and clothing needs he required for his time at sea, a repetition of earlier protestations.

Nelson had decided that his marriage to Fanny had come to an end. He had left her behind in the wake of his human voyage. He was passing out of the normal conventions of the society of his age. The year 1800 had brought Nelson and Emma into the closest connection, and now Horatia had been born, Nelson's legacy. Fanny decided necessarily and no doubt reluctantly to remove herself from the scene; she could not live in close proximity to her husband, Emma and Sir William. She could not remain 'in town', in London, for there was too much gossip there. She took up residence near Brighton. Nelson, now bordering on the callous, cared little about this. To Emma he wrote in terms describing Fanny as a great fool: 'Let her go to Brighton or where she pleases, I care not: she is a great fool and thank God you are not the least like her.' (Vincent 190) Then and afterwards Emma had formed strong and critical opinions about Fanny, and rather cruelly called her that 'vile Tom Tit', which we may interpret as meaning the unwelcome and common bird in the garden. She had also come to dislike Josiah Nisbet.

There was one final, frayed episode of this terribly

traumatic 132 days since the Admiral and his party had stepped ashore at Yarmouth. As Nelson prepared to sail as Second-in-Command of the British fleet destined for Copenhagen, and make his plans to annihilate the Danish fleet lying near Copenhagen, he was anchored in the Downs attending to the pressing, if tedious, business of getting a great armada provisioned, supplied and manned. There was just time to write his last letter to Fanny. She called it 'the letter of dismissal', which indeed it was. It was not just about their broken marital affairs: it was about her son's future in the Navy. Some months earlier, on 15 April 1799, Fanny, aware of her son's ill-natured disposition, had written to him to pay attention to Nelson's requirements as to being a good naval officer worthy of advancement. 'Be assured you are much envied from having such a father to bring you forward, who has every desire to do it.'

Fanny had been badgering him about Josiah. She wanted his preferment. Nelson had obliged, but he was sick to heart of Fanny's importunities on this score.

Now, on the eve of sailing, Josiah, Nelson said, was to have the frigate *Thalia*, or another ship if it could not soon be ready to sail. So, Nelson told Fanny, he had done all he could for her son Josiah. He bared all: he had received little thanks from him in return. In all his relations with Josiah that fellow's friends had stood against Nelson, and now Nelson turned the arguments on his wife: these young men, too, had become his enemies. He told Fanny that, as he had so often done before, Josiah wished only that Nelson would break his own neck. '... therefore my only wish is to be left to myself and wishing you every happiness, believe me that I am your affectionate Nelson and Bronte.' In other words, Nelson wanted to be separated from all promises he had given Fanny with regard to her son's future. The most telling point to be made, and it has not been made previously so far as is known, is that Josiah was 'the cause of the bother'.

It bears remarking that in Nelson's unwritten marriage contract to Fanny he adopted Josiah. He took him to sea. He brought him forth under the considerable influence that he possessed as the greatest rising admiral of the age. All Josiah provided was disappointment to Nelson. He let down his patron. In deferential arrangements obligation existed on both sides. Josiah never acknowledged Nelson's gifts of promotion duly given him. Nelson had fudged the regulations by advancing Josiah ludicrously quickly and in doing so had exposed himself to possible censure and ridicule. Fanny, for her part, never abandoned the quest that her son would do well in the Navy. She looked to Nelson to do as much as he could. Yes, Nelson did as much as he could but Josiah's abilities were not sufficient for the advancement that the famed Admiral provided. Some might call this a demonstration of the 'Peter principle', of someone advanced to the level of their incompetence. Fanny could not understand that her son was not up to the Admiral's expectations. At the end of the day, Nelson had to abandon Josiah, with every good reason. Josiah was uncouth, rude and disloyal to Nelson, a heavy-drinking man who was hardly a credit to his profession as a naval officer. Indeed his behaviour in polite society may not always have been gentlemanly. Nelson was well to be rid of him but it cost him Fanny. Lady Hamilton, too, had done all she could for Josiah, and had loved him in the most sympathetic way. After all, Emma and Josiah were outsiders, in a way. However, Josiah was always a disappointment, but never to himself.

Fanny's friends provided some comfort but the break seemed impossible to mend. One observer, the observant Betsey Wynne Fremantle, whose husband Captain Sir Thomas Fremantle was a close service friend of Nelson's, recorded in her diary on 3 March 1801, 'Lady Nelson is suing for a separate maintenance. I have no patience with her husband, at his age and such a cripple to play the fool with Lady Hamilton.' Matters had changed very quickly, for only four years previously, Betsey Wynne had married Fremantle in Naples. He was with Nelson in the abortive attack on Santa Cruz de Tenerife in July 1797 and brought him home in the frigate *Seahorse*. His wife, who was on board, helped to nurse Nelson.

So closed one of the most difficult periods of Nelson's life, in fact his most difficult year ashore. He was irritable and unhappy. London had left him disconsolate, and since his arrival at Yarmouth it had been a time of intense trial. He wrote to his agent, Alexander Davison, that on reflection he had no desire to return to England under the same circumstances, and rather than live the unhappy life that he had since he last came to England, he would stay abroad forever. But patriotic and naval requirements now brought clarity to his state of mind, and Lord Spencer at the Admiralty knew that Nelson would 'do his part as the Champion of old England.' He knew his naval commander.

As for Josiah, he failed to get the *Thalia*. Nor was another ship given to him. His lieutenant from the *Thalia*, Samuel Colquitt, brought charges against him, apparently sufficient to ruin Josiah's chances. Colquitt was made a Rear-Admiral in 1846. One source of the bother is the fact that Josiah allowed two women to be kept in the gunroom, the midshipmen's room, against regulations. On reflection, it seems that Nelson's most difficult problem in the Navy was Fanny's son Josiah. Josiah was shy, but rowdy ashore with fellow officers, a great contrast to the self-controlled and socially easy Nelson. Josiah lacked social graces and was malevolent. It angered the great sailor that the very person closest to him by family connection and most dependent on his interest or patronage should have proved so cantankerous, so ill-mannered, so lacking in judgment, and so unwilling to pay grateful thanks. Josiah had broken all the rules associated with patronage and advancement in the service. It was he who Alexander Korda identifies as having called Emma 'that Hamilton woman', with derisive connotations. Interest and patronage were the filters of success in the self-selecting processes that took midshipmen to the top as admirals. The spiteful Josiah Nisbet soiled his own nest. The details are not known, but Nelson wrote tantalisingly to Emma of Fanny's ill-treatment of Josiah, an indication that she had become furious with her son at ruining his own chances in the Navy.

And we close the account of Fanny's son, Josiah Nisbet, by noting that he married Frances Herbert Evans in 1819, and died in Paris in 1830. In review, it seems clear that this uncouth fellow was one of the sources of Nelson's alienation from Fanny, and that at the time of the break, 1800, Nelson had made clear to Fanny that he had done as much for Josiah as was possible – and what he had done had been received without thanks. Nelson had done more for Josiah than he should have. Nelson secured a Lieutenancy when he was under 17, a Commandership at 17, and a Post-Captain at a ludicrously young 18. Josiah was undeserving of fast advancement. This was Nelson's error and his embarrassment – but he had kept his contract with Fanny. Josiah never repaid the required deference. Josiah is a shadowy figure in this complex story. He was never cut out to be a naval officer but thrived in the world of investments. Fanny died on 4 May 1831.

Chapter 5 *Nelson and Emma Meet Immortality*

Sir William Hamilton died on 6 April 1803 in Emma's arms, with Nelson holding his hand. Emma owed so much to Sir William, for he had rescued her as a cast-off from Sir Charles Greville. He had taught her in the performances of the Attitudes, had arranged for her lessons in French and Italian, had befriended her and her solicitous mother, Mary Cadogan, and, not least, had married her. In a way, she was his acquisition, but he treated her with all the merits of a great treasure. It goes without saying that he allowed Nelson all the freedom he required with Emma. She was responsible for her own rise to stardom, but in Sir William she had the most remarkable of promoters. Many of the portraits of Emma that survive owe their existence to Sir William's keen sense of Emma's importance, and, naturally, to her connection with the brilliant and rising Admiral. When Sir William died, aged seventy-two, Emma's urbane and sociable patron and protector vanished from the scene. To Nelson he gave a copy of Madame Le Brun's picture of Emma as a small token of high regard for 'the most virtuous, loyal, and truly brave character I ever met with.' Nelson had lost a fine friend.

Shortly thereafter Nelson received orders as Commander-in-Chief of the Mediterranean. He hoisted his flag in the *Victory*. Having reached the height of naval ambition he had had to leave Merton, Emma and Horatia. 'Believe me my dear Emma, although the call of honour separates us, yet my heart is entirely yours and with you.' Emma would have liked to have been with him but that was impossible, as he explained. A portrait of Emma hung in the *Victory*, and Nelson and his private secretary observed a private ritual of drinking a toast to 'our Guardian Angel'.

Others, more so than at any time in his long career, were closely watching Nelson at sea. The Reverend Alexander Scott remarked that Nelson seemed to have a mind free from envy, hatred and malice, and he possessed a sense of charity and a view of the world, and its politics, that set him apart from the men of the world. Nelson's secretary, John Scott, wrote to Emma of the Admiral: 'In my travels through the service I have met with no character equal in any degree to his Lordship', and he went on to praise his quick penetration, clear judgment, great wisdom, correct and decided decisions, his pleasantness of manner and much else. But he forecast, a little worryingly, 'Everyone about him appears more anxious than another for his welfare'. Others observed his constant attention to the health of the officers and men under his command.

Nelson was back with Emma at Merton on 19 August. The delights of a rural England in summer gave rest and repair. There were dashes to London to call on the Admiralty, his agent, to the Prime Minister William Pitt the Younger and the Foreign Secretary Robert Castlereagh. He was mobbed when in town, the subject of wonder and admiration. At Merton he and Emma were flooded with visitors. Then it was back to sea – and for the very last time.

The Battle of Trafalgar, 21 October 1805, was the ruination of the French and Spanish fleets. It secured British maritime supremacy for the rest of the war against Napoleon. It bought on much sorrow for all the participants. The bells of victory rang only in the British Isles and in the British Empire.

'Trafalgar was', wrote Vice-Admiral Cuthbert Collingwood three months after the event, 'the cause of far more lamentation than joy. Never did a man's death cause so universal a sorrow as Lord Nelson's.' Nelson's Second-in-Command, known for his icy reserve, wept when he was given the news. 'My heart is rent', he wrote the next day, 'with most poignant grief for the death of a friend, to whom ... I was bound by the strongest ties of affection.' All who had been there on the day, or in the battle generally, felt bereft of an idol, and they took the loss as a personal one. A young seaman in the *Royal*

Sovereign wrote:

> Our dear Admiral Nelson is killed! .... I never set eyes
> on him, for which I am sorry and glad; for to be sure I
> should like to have seen him, but then, all the men in
> our ship who have seen him are such soft toads, they
> have done nothing but Blast their eyes and cry ever
> since he was killed. God bless you! Chaps that fought
> like the Devil, sit down and cry like a wench.

In England, Lady Nelson received official regrets from
Lord Barham, First Lord of the Admiralty:

> Madam, it is with the utmost concern that, in the midst
> of victory, I have to inform your Ladyship of the death
> of your illustrious partner, Lord Viscount Nelson. After
> leading the British fleet into close action with the
> enemy and seeing their defeat, he fell by a musket ball
> entering his chest. It is the death he wished for and
> less to be regretted on his own account. But the public
> loss is irretrievable. I can only add that events of this
> kind do not happen by chance. I recommend therefore
> your Ladyship to His protection, who is alone able to
> save, or to destroy.

Emma was at Merton when news reached her of the
death of Nelson. Five weeks had passed since she had
last seen him. When Nelson's final letter, written 19
October, and found open on his desk, had been received
at Merton, she wrote upon it, 'Oh miserable, wretched
Emma. Oh glorious and happy Nelson.' Nelson had

Ah where, & ah where, is my gallant Sailor gone?
He's gone to Fight the Frenchmen, for George upon the Throne.
DIDO, in Despair!
He's gone to fight ye Frenchmen, t'loose t'other Arm & Eye,
And left me with the old Antiques, to lay me down & Cry.

34. Gillray's cruel portrayal of a distraught and monstrously fat Emma following Nelson's departure for sea in 1801 takes for its reference Virgil's *Aeneid* and adds further farce by allusion to her Attitudes. Sir William's useless classical objects, turned here into phallic symbols, are strewn around her.

35. Supposedly worked by Emma, this
embroidered picture shows Emma and Nelson
together with Merton Place in the background.
Only in the autumn of 1805, after Hamilton's
death in 1803, did they enjoy time
together with Horatia.

36. Merton Place was bought by Nelson in 1801 and became the home of the *ménage à trois* of Emma, Nelson and, somewhat neglected, the ageing Hamilton. Nelson was delighted with Merton, and in September 1805 Emma wrote 'now he is here 'tis a paradise.'

37. The shocking death of Nelson following the victory off Cap
Trafalgar generated simple prints such as this. Emma was
inconsolable. Nelson's last private act before the battle, the writing
of a codicil to his will in which he beseeched the King and Country
to look after Emma and Horatia, was never honoured.

38. Gillray's print of Nelson's death shows him fatally wounded on deck with a winged figure above proclaiming his imminent immortality. The grieving personification of Britannia can be no other than Emma

39. The Grand funeral car that carried Nelson's body from the
Admiralty to St Paul's Cathedral. His committal was followed
by Handel's chorus, 'His body is buried in peace – but
his name liveth evermore.'

40. In Benjamin West's allegorical painting of 1807, Nelson's
immortality was given full expression in this apotheosis.
For Emma, however, the future held only debt, drink and
a sad and lonely death in Calais in 1815, her ministrations
to Nelson and to her country unrecognised.

41. In Horatia the great affair lived on, and in this portrait of 1815 the young daughter is shown with a pendant in which can be spotted a miniature portrait of her father.

written: 'My dearest Emma, the dear friend of my bosom, the Signal has been made that the Enemy's combined fleet are coming out of port ... May God Almighty give us success over these fellows and enable us to get a Peace.'

Nelson's correspondence, to Emma and to others, save Fanny in later years when the correspondence became legal and brittle, shows generosity of spirit and the inspiration that inspired devotion in others. His letters, as Oliver Warner rightly concludes, 'will remain an inspiration to all who share his eternal eagerness to serve his country, and to those who – in the words of his beloved Emma – "can never be a lukewarm friend".'

The state passed out its rewards, some to Fanny but none to Emma. Nelson's brother William was made an Earl and was given a fortune, allowing him to live in undeserved splendour. Fanny did not attend the funeral at St Paul's but a coach was arranged so that the windows were drawn down to show that it was empty.

As for Emma, she received no invitation, and we do not know where she spent the day, but it is certain that she spent it in abject despair. Some days later her friend Lady Elizabeth Foster (connected to the Duke and Duchess of Devonshire, for she and the Duchess had the Duke in common) called on her at Merton and reported:

I found her in bed. She had the appearance of a person stunned and scarcely as yet able to comprehend the certainty of her loss. 'What shall I do?' and 'How can I exist?' were her first words ... 'Days have passed on and I know not how they end or begin – nor how I am to bear my future existence'.

Nelson had left Emma, as he put it, 'as a legacy for my King and Country.' By this he meant that he expected that the state would look after her in the future. It was a vain hope. His will gave her the freehold of Merton, a legacy of £2000, and an annuity of £500. This was insufficient.

She entertained lavishly, expenditures never being met, and before long, despite help and advice from friends, she was facing insurmountable debt. In 1813 she was arrested for debt, and was consigned to Southwark prison, though allowed on parole to live with Horatia in nearby lodgings. She called out for money, and got assistance from a number of persons. For instance, from Earl Nelson, Horatio's brother, additional funds were made to her annuity. This allowed her to escape to Calais, and she and Horatia lived in squalid upper rooms at 27 rue Française. By 1814 the end was drawing near for Emma. That year a box of letters Nelson had written to her somehow fell into mercenary hands, and the contents published against her objections. Even before this, her secretary, Francis Oliver threatened publication of Nelson's letters to her, truly a case of blackmail against an ailing and increasingly defenceless victim. She died on 15 January 1815, probably from liver disease. Her wealth at death was 15 francs, with clothes valued at 200 francs. She was buried in Calais, the wooden cross marking her grave bore the epitaph 'Emma Hamilton, England's friend'.

As for Horatia she was taken home to England by the British Consul and placed in the care of Nelson's sister and brother-in-law, Kate and George Matcham, and later with his sister's family, the Boltons. She married the curate of Burnham Market, Norfolk, Philip Ward, and had a large family. To the end, she did not acknowledge Emma as her mother, despite strong evidence. However, she knew that Nelson was her father: he had told her so in a legal document.

'Emma Hamilton', concluded Tom Pocock, 'was more than a colourful character and a foil to the greatest naval commander and popular hero in the long war with revolutionary and Napoleonic France. She inspired Nelson, and if her influence was at time baleful, as at Naples in 1799, she played her part in forming his sense of destiny, which lifted his conduct as a commander and a national figure to great heights at the climax of his life that ended in his victory at Trafalgar.' That is a fair assessment from an historian known for sober judgments.

Emma provided Nelson's inspiration in his greatest hours of need and finest hours of achievement. During all those long days at sea, in all the preparations for battle, including the last epochal hour, thoughts of 'dear Emma' were near the forefront of his mind. He cherished her supreme powers in the arts of love and affection, and these he needed so desperately and without qualification. She had given him the supreme gift that yielded inspiration, and that in turn found reflection in the 'Band of Brothers' born so heroically in the officers and men of the Royal Navy at Trafalgar. He laid aside the conventions of the age in forging this union with Lady Hamilton. Her impulsive theatricality and affectionate nature ruled his passions, fed his vanity, and fuelled his recognition of the importance of duty. 'Duty is the great business of a sea officer,' he advised, 'all private considerations must give way to it however painful it is.' Horatio, Lord Nelson knew of that pain, expressed so clearly in his correspondence and life with Emma. There was only one Emma as there was only one Nelson. It may seem to be one of the most improbable unions of history, and for certain it is one of the great love affairs. On reflection, it is hard to imagine a Nelson without an Emma.

Such an appreciation, which to this age now seems eminently sensible, and is worthy of repeated applause, did not exist at that time. Emma, fallen from all grace and favour, remained a shadowy figure, caught up in scandal. She was also a person marginalised from history – a distraction, even embarrassment, to the Nelson legacy and the legend of the great conquering Admiral. Even on the centenary of the Battle of Trafalgar in 1905 she was pushed to the background. Her biographers treated her either as an embarrassment irrelevant to the story, or a platonic friend of their subject. Victorian reticence was part of it, and this seems to have built itself on a prudery that existed, surprisingly enough, in the late eighteenth and early nineteenth centuries, and is often discounted nowadays. The malicious and scurrilous *Memoirs of Lady Hamilton,* published anonymously not long after her death, were no help to her reputation, and even Horatia's reluctance to acknowledge Emma as her mother did little to redeem her in the public's eyes. Almost a century later the views had changed, for Emma's correspondence brought the relationship with Nelson into perspective. Serious biographers set to work, and placed her more agreeably in time and space – and, important to our theme, showed her as a stimulant to the genius of Nelson.

She was the most remarkable of the 'women behind the fleet'. She was, too, an important foil and, most remarkable of all, a forceful character in her own right. It is altogether suitable as well as natural that hers is a story for all the ages – of a heroine engaged in a remarkable love affair with England's genius of sea battles. Say what you will, Emma had time on her side, and she grows in our appreciation by the minute.

Sources *Writing Emma and Nelson*

Indicative of Emma's claim on the fascinations of her contemporaries is the sizeable literature that appeared about her at the time, or shortly after, her death. This, however, is to say nothing of those works that couple her fascinating career and escapades with those of Nelson. In all there is inseparability – of two lives caught up in destiny's unfolding. Included here are some of the best-published works of recent times, the cream of a sizeable and engrossing body of literature.

Lives of Emma
Kate Williams' *England's Mistress*: *The Infamous Life of Emma Hamilton* (2007) sets the new standard for absorbing, well-researched works not only of the iconic Emma but of enduring female characters of that age.

Walter Sichel, *Emma Lady Hamilton* (1905) provided a sympathetic portrait emblematic of its age. Julia Frankau's *Nelson's Legacy* (1910) offered an inspired appreciation of Emma's early life and later tragic progressions. Norah Lofts, *Emma Hamilton* (1979) is a handsome biography, beautifully illustrated as befits its subject. The same can be said for the nuanced *Beloved Emma*, by Flora Fraser (1998).

For a brief life with a thorough guide to documentary sources, see the online entry 'Hamilton [nee Lyon], Emma, Lady Hamilton', *Oxford Dictionary of National Biography*.

Much is to be gained from the newer literature on women and the Navy in the late eighteenth and early nineteenth centuries, of which Margarette Lincoln's *Naval Wives & Mistresses* (2008) sets a high standard. See also, Amanda Vickery, *The Gentleman's Daughter: Women's Lives in Georgian England* (1998). A sympathetic, non-judgemental account of Emma and the 1799 Neopolitan revolution is Marjorie Bowen's *Patriotic Lady* (1935). Portraits of Emma inspire the present book but have induced others to mount exhibitions – for example, the Arts Council exhibition at Kenwood House, Hampstead Heath. See, in this connection, *Lady Hamilton in Relation to the Art of her Time* (catalogue of the exhibition, 1972).

New discoveries continue to be made. See Peter Hore and Michael Nash, 'Emma and the Mimoplastic Art', in *Trafalgar Chronicle 25* (The 1805 Club, 2015), which prints for the first time for more than a century the alluring *From the Nude*, Romney's *c*1782–86 depiction, with Emma probably at the height of her sexual powers. (Plate 8)

Lives of Nelson

Robert Southey will always be first in the hearts of many seeking a brief biography of the naval hero, for his *Life of Nelson* was published, in 1813, not long after Trafalgar. In Southey's 1854 edition Nelson's own memoir of his services, compiled in 1800 for the *Naval Chronicle*, appeared as an appendix within the same covers of this enduring portrait. Nelson is a naval hero for all ages, and given the fact that ten years still existed between his death and Waterloo not surprisingly many a biography or other appreciation occurred as a stir to the supremely maritime nation to fulfill its destiny and defeat the power of France under Napoleon. Nelson's star did not diminish in the long years of *Pax Britannica*, and many a British admiral serving as Commander-in-Chief on a faraway station of the Royal Navy had served under Nelson and preserved 'the immortal memory' in word and song, and particularly at the annual celebration of Trafalgar Day. Captain Jack Aubrey's veneration of Nelson in the Patrick O'Brian historical novels, and shown in Peter Weir's film *Master and Commander* (2003), is no understatement, and to this day, on Trafalgar Day, any wardroom of a ship of the Royal Navy, or any Commonwealth navy, will find a toast being raised to 'The Immortal Memory'.

Although the United States naval officer Alfred Thayer Mahan is best known for his *Influence of Sea Power upon History* trilogy, his *The Life of Nelson, The Embodiment of British Sea Power*, first published, 1897, is remarkable as witness to the life of Nelson. It has extraordinary insights into Emma, and from the position of a high Anglican or Episcopalian, true appreciation and sympathy for the personal difficulties of the naval hero and the courtesan. The first edition brought reprisals, and in the second edition (and after) Mahan strengthened his sympathies and his understandings. The second revised edition (2001, with an introduction by Pieter van der Merwe) is recommended.

Oliver Warner's *Portrait of Lord Nelson* (1958), a favourite among those interested in well-written appreciations, combines erudition with sympathy for the subject – essential for great biography. See also, his *Emma Hamilton and Sir William* (1960). Carola Oman's *Nelson* (1947), a classic, has been justly reprinted. Tom Pocock's *Horatio Nelson* (1987) provides an erudite appreciation of a complex character driven to fame and to fortune and to death. Pocock shows why people loved Nelson and venerate him to this day. These biographies of Nelson were mere warm-ups to the big events offered by the publishing industry.

The 2005 bicentenary of the Battle of Trafalgar sparked a flurry of interest and a flourishing output of biographies by leading British naval historians and biographers, notably Roger Knight's magisterial *The Pursuit of Victory: The Life and Achievement of Horatio Nelson* (2005) – which shows that Nelson had a keen political sense but was often a difficult subordinate. It is strong on naval operations. Andrew Lambert's finely drawn portrait *Nelson: Britannia's God of War* (2004) vividly and thoroughly examines strategy, tactics, logistics and operations.

John Sugden's *Nelson* (2004, 2012) shows that even to this day much new material continues to surface on the life and times of Nelson – and Emma.

Edgar Vincent, *Nelson: Love and Fame* (2003) explains the all-consuming affair with Emma. Altogether these works provided scholarly detachment with understandable appreciation for the life and times of the hero – and the heroine.

Many a reprint of the classic works appeared in 2005 or at about this time, too, giving added credence to the appreciations of yesteryear. A favourite of many, William Clark Russell's *Pictures from the Life of Nelson*, first published in 1897, has the flavour of a number of spritely articles written for an English magazine, and indeed that is the case. Not true biography it is a far better life of Nelson than Clark Russell's heavily ballasted biography of Nelson, which as one authority unerringly put it, would have been settling well below the Plimsoll line if leaving port. 2005 was a banner year for Nelson studies but it benefitted those dealing with Emma, for as they say, 'all boats rise on the same tide'.

On leadership, Arthur Marder, '*The Art of Leadership: Nelson, a Case Study*,' *Naval Review*, 49 (October 1961): 124-32, is a good beginning. Marder follows Ludovic Kennedy's line that before, and for too long, the men serving in the Navy had survived from two types of commanders: aristocrats and, later, the 'tarpaulins', that rough breed who had little understanding of human nature or life's more refined aspects. Nelson was pre-eminent among the new type of officer, distinguished from their predecessors on account of their respect for the dignity of the individual. Nelson championed the improvement of the lower deck's living conditions, and he placed health, mental and physical, as top require-ments for life on board a man-of-war.

Nelson, indeed, was exceptional for his leadership – and also for the example he gave to others who fought with him or who, later, sought to emulate him. On these and other matters, see Peter Hore's *Nelson's Band of Brothers* (Seaforth, in association with The 1805 Club, 2015).

The interlocking lives of Emma and Nelson

For a beginning, see Tom Pocock's *Nelson's Women* (1999), noted above. An all-time favourite is Roger Hudson's *Nelson and Emma* (Folio Society 1994), a compilation of letters and other appreciations blended beautifully into a narrative of absorbing power.

Nelson's fame has always been haunted as well as blessed by the notoriety of his relations with women. Emma and Fanny were only the most prominent, and Tom Pocock in *Nelson's Women* first exposed, with clarity, how, serially, Nelson passed from the loving arms of one woman to another – with various degrees of success and with much heartbreak. Pocock also illuminates the life of Nelson's mother, who fell in love and married her social inferior, herself dying young. None of this diminishes Emma's powers of fascination over England's Glory and tells a great deal of the psychological desire of need that so moved Nelson.

Miscellany

The lives and perils of Emma and Nelson can be followed in their letters, and in correspondence of others about them. This was a letter-writing age, and letters were far more important than autobiography or memoir. Thus we have a very large shelf of books of letters of these two very large personages. New letters continue to appear at auction, or in attics, and thus we have the most recent collection, Colin White's edition *Nelson: The New Letters* (2005), published in association with the National Maritime Museum and The Royal Navy Museum. White presented 507 new letters and some other items. It is tempting to say that there will be other similar works, but perhaps one day a scholarly collection along the lines of the Disraeli or Gladstone correspondence may see the light of day. 'That there should still be letters to be added to the corpus already in existence would seem a miracle', says the dust jacket of White's compilation, but the *Nelson Letter Project* added material relating to family, also some secret materials, and details from official papers. As they say, 'truth will out', and it is thus with Emma and Nelson. Sad to say, Nelson burned Emma's letters to him, fearing that if they were discovered she would be exposed to ridicule and abuse, even to the legal charge of 'alienation of affection'. White's *Nelson: The New Letters* also offers a useful guide to all the collections of Emma and Nelson.

Nelson's Purse, by Martin Downer, published 2002, reveals that treasures are to be found even at this late hour– and in unlikely places. Searching in a Swiss castle for jewels to put on auction in London, he chanced on a dispatch box of Nelson letters and other items. A greater appreciation of Fanny is given, as the long-suffering and alienated wife.

On Lady Nelson, see the first biography devoted to this little-known and under-appreciated viscountess, E.M. Keate, *Nelson's Wife* (1939).

Brian Fothergill's *Sir William Hamilton* (1969) is a workable study, as is Oliver Warner's *Emma Hamilton and Sir William* (1960). Susan Sontag's *Volcano Lover* (1992) is irresistible as an examination of the role of antiquities as a social construct of that erudite age. This book is also about revolution, the fate of nature, and the condition of women. It is also one of the greatest examples of creative non-fiction.

Winifred Gérin's *Horatia Nelson* (1970) is a scholarly work of fascination and merit, bringing dimension to the story of Emma and Nelson's only known surviving kin.

The beginning point for any serious student of this subject, or for that matter, the dilettante or the inquisitive, is *Nelson's Letters to his Wife and Other Documents, 1785-1831*, published by the esteemed Navy

Records Society (1958) and edited by George PB Naish of The National Maritime Museum. More than the title indicates, the work includes Fanny's importunate letters to Nelson and his 'letter of dismissal'. It also includes some of Sir William Hamilton's letters to Nelson about Emma.

Author Biographies

BARRY GOUGH was professor of history at Wilfrid Laurier University in Ontario until retirement in 2004. An expert on the maritime history of the Pacific Ocean, he has published widely on Anglo-Canadian naval subjects. His dual biography, *Historical Dreadnoughts Marder and Roskill*, was published by Seaforth in 2010. He has also contributed the new introductions to Arthur Marder's seminal work, the five-volume *From the Dreadnought to Scapa Flow*, also published by Seaforth.

ARTHUR J MARDER, born in 1910, became perhaps the most distinguished historian of the modern Royal Navy. He held a number of teaching posts in American universities and published some fifteen major works on British naval history. As well as his five-volume history of the RN in the First World War Seaforth Publishing have also released his *From the Dardanelles to Oran* and *Operation Menace*.

For more details of these and other Seaforth titles visit our website: www.seaforthpublishing.com